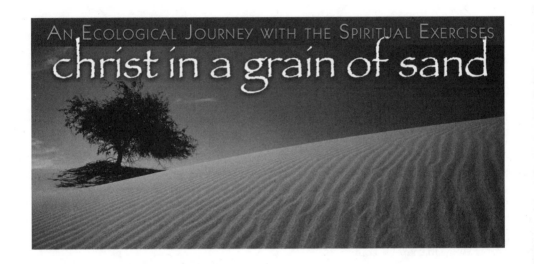

AN ECOLOGICAL JOURNEY WITH THE SPIRITUAL EXERCISES

christ in a grain of sand

NEIL VANEY, SM

FOREWARD BY WILLIAM A. BARRY, S.J.

ave maria press AMP Notre Dame, Indiana

© 2004 by Ave Maria Press, Inc.

www.avemariapress.com

International Standard Book Number: 0-59471-017-1

Cover and text design by Brian Conley

Printed and bound in the United States of America.

Library of Congress Cataloging-in-Publication Data

Vaney, Neil.
  Christ in a grain of sand : an ecological journey with the Spiritual exercises / Neil Vaney ; foreword by William A. Barry.
     p. cm.
  Includes bibliographical references.
  ISBN 1-59471-017-1 (pbk.)
  1. Ignatius, of Loyola, Saint, 1491-1556. Exercitia spiritualia. 2. Human ecology--Religious aspects--Christianity. 3. Ecology--Religious aspects--Christianity. I. Title.

  BX2179.L8V36 2004
  248.3--dc22

                              2004010021

CONTENTS

ACKNOWLEDGMENTS

The writing of this book has taken place mainly in two intensive writing periods spread over the last three years. In other ways, it is the distillation of a lifetime's reflection and prayer. Particularly since writing my doctoral thesis in the area of environmental ethics and the theology of nature at the University of Otago, New Zealand, my thought has crystallized around the parallels between the universe story and Jesus' story as presented in St. Ignatius's *Spiritual Exercises*. My teaching of theology in Auckland from 1994 to 2003 has given me the chance to read numerous books and articles on theology and science and has allowed these thoughts to become more firmly integrated.

My deep gratitude goes to the Society of Mary for the freedom and space to work on this study, and for my teaching institute, Good Shepherd College, for the time away from teaching needed to write this book. I owe a particular debt to the Basilean priests and parishioners of St. Mark's in Vancouver, who hosted me during my writing during the second half of 1999. Similarly I thank my colleagues at the Catholic Institute of Sydney, who provided me with a superb environment for writing in the summer of 2003. Many personal friends going back to my time as chaplain at the University of Canterbury (1973–77) have given me warm support during this time as well.

I must take the opportunity also to thank sincerely the Jesuits I have come to know and who have been so helpful to me in my efforts to present my reading of Ignatius of Loyola for the twenty-first century. Thank you for your openness and commitment to the vision of Ignatius.

FOREWORD

I was once told of a mysterious statement by one of the ancient rabbis. "You cannot tell the story of Genesis to more than three people at a time." On the face of it, it is false. You can tell the story to any number of people at a time. In fact, the story is read to hundreds at a time in synagogues and churches around the world. So the statement requires reflection. Why was it preserved in the Mishnah? Its mystery resolves itself when you realize that the story meant is the story behind the story in the Book of Genesis. Before God said, "Let there be . . ." there is nothing, nothing at all except God. In her remarkable poem "Primary Wonder," Denise Levertov touches on the great mystery that there is "anything at all, let alone cosmos, joy, memory, everything/ rather than void. . . ." The history of spirituality is a record of the human effort to come to terms with such primary wonder. It is a history of human astonishment that human beings exist at all, that, indeed, anything exists and also a history of human answers to the questions that flow from this astonishment: Why does anything exist? What does God want? What does it mean to exist in this vast universe? What is our place in it? What do we human beings want?

The Bible indicates that the Mystery we call God, who is the creator of this universe, has created human beings for friendship—with God, with one another, and with the whole created universe. Human beings are, astonishingly, made in the image of God, a God who is intrinsically relational, as we discovered through reflection on the mystery of the life, death, and resurrection of Jesus of Nazareth. God creates us to invite us to become sharers of God's relational life. Indeed, we are invited to share in God's creative intentions for our world. The Bible also indicates, almost on every page, that God's desire for friendship with us and for our cooperation in God's work in this world continually seems to be thwarted by human folly and sin. How are we to find our way back to what God wants, given all the siren songs that derive from human folly and sin? Various spiritualities are responses to this question.

Ignatius of Loyola, in the sixteenth century, offered a way to discover an answer to the question, a way that he distilled in his classic *Spiritual Exercises*. This little book, a manual for the director of the exercises contained in the book, has been found helpful by millions of people in the four centuries since its first publication. Ignatius presumes that God continually communicates with each human being, trying to draw each one into friendship and cooperation. His exercises are offered as a means to pay attention to this self-communicating God and to try to align one's life in accord with what God wants.

Ignatius, like everyone else, was a man of his time and culture. His worldview was developed at the cusp that marked the end of the medieval synthesis and the beginning of the modern era. Is his spiritual way still viable in our world, especially in the worldview spawned by the discoveries of modern science that have so greatly expanded our knowledge of the immensity of the universe and the interconnectedness of everything in it?

In this fine book Neil Vaney, a Marist priest from New Zealand, answers in the affirmative. For many years he has been involved in using *The Spiritual Exercises* in his own country and elsewhere. His own studies in environmental ethics and the theology of nature have given him a breathtakingly broad grasp of scientific theories and discoveries without taking him away from the heart of the spiritual quest, which is the need for personal answers to the meaning of one's place in this vast universe. This book is a labor of love, love of God, love of God's creation, and love of the way blazed over four centuries ago by Ignatius of Loyola. Directors of the Exercises and those who make them will profit from the book and find Fr. Vaney's explanations of scientific discoveries eye-opening and very helpful. His insights prove, once again, that Ignatius's little book is a gift to the whole church and is not a preserve of the Society of Jesus. From one admirer of Ignatius to another, my thanks go out to Neil Vaney. I hope that this book reaches a wide audience.

William A. Barry, S.J.

INTRODUCTION

The first question which you will ask and which I must
try to answer is this, "What is the use of climbing
Mount Everest?" and my answer must at once be, "It is
no use." There is not the slightest prospect of any gain
whatsoever. . . . We shall not bring back a single piece of
gold or silver, not a gem, nor any coal or iron. . . . It's no
use. So, if you cannot understand that there is something in man which responds to the challenge of this
mountain and goes out to meet it, that the struggle is the
struggle of life itself upward and forever upward, then
you won't see why we go. What we get from this adventure is just sheer joy. And joy is, after all, the end of life.
We eat and make money to be able to enjoy life. That is
what life means and what life is for.

George Mallory died on the northeast ridge of Mount Everest somewhere above twenty-eight thousand feet in 1924. It was his third expedition to the world's highest peak, and he had been reluctant to leave
his wife and new job at Cambridge. What drew him ultimately was joy,
the joy he describes in his interview. Elements of that joy are identical
to what we read in the accounts of the experience of the prophets on
mountaintops like Sinai. For the ancient Israelites, a mountaintop was
the threshold of the abode of God. As the prophet gazed down the
tumbling valleys, the people's smallness and the prophet's own fragility
came into sharp perspective. Amid the stark beauty of the heights, the
links between God, humankind, and nature are razor sharp. Humbled,
dwarfed, stripped of all pretensions on the tops, the prophets descended from the heights with faces aglow (Moses; see Ex 34:29) or they

sprinted for miles in exultation on the crest of the storm (Elijah; see 1 Kgs 18:46). For the prophets and for us, to see God on the mountain is to know joy.

It is my hope that this book will provide for the reader a similar mountaintop experience. As we climb, our senses will be focused in two directions. We focus first on God, whose word may whisper in our ears in any unmarked cave where we shelter. And then we focus on the shattered rock sliding down the scree slopes and the lichen-encrusted walls of the narrow stone chimneys where we brace our feet as we make our ascent. An immense respect for both God and nature will mark our journey, for like the prophets we will discover them to be mirror images of each other. Our guide on this journey will be Ignatius of Loyola and our Baedeker the route he sketched in *The Spiritual Exercises*. Like Mallory, we may never reach the summit. Then again, no one knows how high he climbed. For each climber, the personal summit may differ. It is the experience of climbing that matters. The experience of the body's tiredness, the rediscovery of the vitality in this primal world, and the astonishing perspectives opening up below one's feet all bring joy. Much of Mallory's fame rests on that fact he died on his final journey. Like him, we too risk death—death to stunted images of God, to smug utilitarian views of the relationship between humankind and the rest of creation, to predetermined boundary lines about where God's presence abides, and to a diminished sense of personal and cosmic history. As we die on our pilgrimage with Ignatius, we may feel both a keen loss and a quickening of new life and freedom within us.

Using This Book

As we begin this journey, some knowledge of *The Spiritual Exercises* of St. Ignatius can be helpful. Readers who have made a thirty-day retreat or have followed the retreat in daily life (the so-called Nineteenth Annotation) will find that this book follows the same path. The work could also be used as a complementary text for either retreatant or director in the actual course of making the Exercises for the first time.

But one need not have already had these experiences to take this journey. Like the Nineteenth Annotation, *Christ in a Grain of Sand* is in itself a way of making the Exercises with a particular consciousness. You could work with a guide who has made the Exercises. For many people, family and work commitments or physical circumstances make it virtually impossible to make a long retreat. In that situation, reading this book prayerfully could be a first step in love and hope to a time when it is possible to enter personally into a fuller experience of the Exercises.

This book is designed as a commentary following the structure of the Exercises, that is, four "weeks" or periods, each focusing on a progressive imitation and identification by the retreatant with a particular stage of Christ's journey from birth to death. The normal division is: the fundamental choices and preparation for the journey (Week One); Jesus' birth, life, and public ministry (Week Two); his suffering and death (Week Three); his resurrection and new life (Week Four). Thirty days of intensive prayer and reflection are usually regarded as the norm for the full Exercises. I will follow that convention. The reflections I propose to the reader try to highlight the ecological and natural values that underlie each stage of the journey. They attempt to illustrate how such a multileveled reading of the text illuminates and opens up the traditional reading to a much wider experience of understanding and conversion.

Readers may use this work in a variety of different ways. Particular insights as to how God works in parallel ways in nature and in the spiritual life may be so fruitful that readers might want to savor and ruminate on them for as long as the insight provides stimulus for prayer and reflection. Other readers may wish to use the book as a liturgical prayer resource. For instance, the second week could serve as a source for prayer and meditation during the time of Advent. Week Four, focusing on Jesus' risen life, would make a rich prayer resource during the Easter-Pentecost season. Or one could use the book in the traditional way as a step-by-step companion to the Exercises, whether made over thirty days, six months, or even a year.

Because this book is a prayerful reflection on the rightful place of humans within creation, it requires an experience of the reader's whole being, body and spirit, embodied in—as well as transforming and being transformed by—nature. Prayer and meditation are critical for this process. They act as barriers against the flood of seductive sensory messages that bombard us from advertising, visual media, and brand projection at every waking moment of our day. To awaken instead the echoes of God's creative spirit in us, we who pray and reflect need to shape the fruit of our deliberations into structures that resonate with clarity, power, and beauty. Simply recording them in a journal or notebook begins this process. Sharing our new vision with a prayer companion, a prayer group, or a small Christian community is a further stage in the re-creation of meaning. Expressing this in poetry, in paint or clay, or even in music allows us to share even further in God's creative wisdom. To complete the cycle, we need physical and practical expressions to underline and embody our convictions. Planting and cultivating a garden, reclaiming roadsides or vacant land in a run-down neighborhood, joining a hiking or conservation group, exploring political options to fight against exploitation of workers in sweatshops—all of these are further steps to renew God's creative work in our world. Creating something beautiful is a gateway to discovering God as the source and sustainer of all that is beautiful in our universe.

Following the Movements

This work is something like an orchestral symphony in five movements. The opening movement, the introduction, serves to preview all the themes that will be heard in the four weeks. It contains many insights and values that will progressively be explored and expanded in the rest of the book. It sketches a brief spiritual vision of the way that God, the human spirit, and the world of nature can best interact, a vision that the attentive reader will recognize growing and developing throughout the rest of the book. The other chapters move through the movements, which for the sake of conciseness I will label as: opening to God's gifts; birth and epiphany; death to illusion; and rising to new life. Each movement will consist of a number of short subjects.

This book follows the traditional practice of identifying the movements as weeks and the themes within them as days. These are not weeks in the literal sense, since some weeks have as many as ten days or as few as five. The reader should feel no compulsion to finish a week in seven days, or even to move from one day to the next following a calendar. Rather, move at the pace that seems best, perhaps dwelling longer than a day on a theme that has particular importance.

Apart from a couple of minor alterations, the development of each week will follow the order of meditations, exercises, and spiritual reflections that Ignatius himself finally settled upon as the shape of *The Spiritual Exercises*. Each theme for prayer and reflection, for example, the sin of the angels, or Peter walking on the sea of Galilee, will be introduced by a prayer desire (to stress the particular grace that the retreatant is seeking in this reflection) and by an Ignatian focus (a brief citation from Ignatius's own text) to locate this reflection in the saint's own structure. I have avoided a literal translation of Ignatius and tried to paraphrase in modern language. The scriptural passages are prefaced with a brief theological reflection coupled with an ecological theme or parallel suggested by that episode. After the scriptural passage that is the main source of prayer follows a brief commentary that attempts to use the work of modern scholars to shed light on and help place the passage in the context of the early communities for which these texts were written.

After each passage I have added a few questions that hopefully will stimulate the reader's awareness, helping to make links between God's action as portrayed in the scriptures, in nature, and in the reader's own life. Some of these will try to deepen the sense of God's action throughout every realm of creation. Finally, each theme will conclude with a prayer, a poem, or a reflection that encapsulates the core of this moment to be relished and taken as food for the continuing journey.

PRAYER DESIRE	Identifies the particular grace that we seek in this reflection
IGNATIAN FOCUS	A brief citation from *The Spiritual Exercises*
INTRODUCTION	A brief introduction to the theme of the day.
ECOLOGICAL REFLECTION	An ecological theme or parallel is suggested
SCRIPTURE REFLECTION	A passage suggested for reading and reflection
SCRIPTURE COMMENTARY	A brief explanation of the reading
ADDITIONAL PASSAGES	More related scripture passages

QUESTIONS FOR REFLECTION	Connects scripture, nature, and our own lives
A FINAL THOUGHT	A prayer, a poem, or a reflection that encapsulates the core of this moment to be relished and taken as food for the continuing journey

To Hold Infinity in the Palm of Your Hand

In the early days of my own thirty-day retreat, an image of myself as a seven-year-old surfaced from my memory. I had seen it briefly in a family photo album many years before. It showed me as a tiny, gaunt, freckled kid hugging my knees as I sat on the back lawn of a neighbor's house. Over the next three weeks the significance of that snapshot grew daily within me. It opened up themes of being different, of being alone, as well as memories of loving mother substitutes; it set me once more among the houses, lawns, parks, and hills of Karori, Wellington, where I grew up, which was home. It brought me back to the deepest questions of identity and belonging.

The following chapter seeks to awake many such images in you. It attempts to bring you to your own home, your mother earth, this planet, and to begin to see it with fresh eyes. Its goal is to open your gaze to see sky, trees, rocks, and rivers in previously unimagined ways. Seeing with new eyes, you will be ready to see Jesus—the cosmic child and Lord of creation—anew in the four weeks of *The Spiritual Exercises*.

Theme 1.
God's Constant Creation

One of the key teachings of the Bible is that God is faithful. Heaven and earth may pass away, but God's word does not waver. In the first verse of the first book of the Hebrew scriptures we are told that God initiates the word of love that calls everything into being. A number of Jewish commentators believe that this phrase is more correctly translated, "When God began to create . . ." or "In the beginning of God's creation . . ." (Gn 1:1). They point to ancient Jewish stories that God shaped many other universes before fixing on this one because it met the desires of his heart. When Jesus appeared to his disciples in the upper room after his resurrection, he breathed on them and promised them the Spirit as a pledge of forgiveness for their betrayal of him (Jn 20:22). He creates the world anew in evoking the first word of love that God breathed, assuring them that the apparent triumph of darkness was only a passing phase in God's love story for this universe. God is in the risen Christ refashioning a new creation.

Most present day scripture scholars believe that the creation account we read in the first two chapters of the Book of Genesis is actually a composite of two accounts from different sources. The first, Gn 1:1–2:4a, is the more recent and was probably composed by a group of priestly writers in Babylon about the time of the Jewish deportation in the sixth century B.C. It stresses the uniqueness of Yahweh, his ordering and control of all of creation. The second and older account was gradually compiled from very ancient sources perhaps three or four centuries earlier. Both accounts, but especially the priestly narrative, stress that God's love sustains everything in being: without that all else would vanish; only God would endure. After God's anger at human sinfulness has been unleashed in the great flood described in Gn 7:6–9:17, Yahweh reaffirms his everlasting pledge to sustain the earth and all on it when he recommits himself to a new covenant whose pledge is the rainbow: "When the bow is in the clouds, I will look upon it and remember the everlasting covenant between God and every living creature of all flesh that is on the earth" (Gn 9:16). This covenant is addressed not just to humans but to all creatures on earth. God assures the Jewish people he will never revoke the blessing of existence. This stance is in strong contrast to many of the contemporaneous Babylonian creation myths in which the gods plot to destroy humankind and the world.

There is another sense in which God never ceases to create. Creation is a continual process that is being played out in every rock and stream, every mountain and sea on our planet. This is not so much a bringing something out of nothing as it is a constant balancing act that prevents the forces and dynamics hidden within the earth from destroying the elaborate network of life that festoons the planet. To see these dynamics is to open one's eyes to a new comprehension of the world.

Nowhere do we see this process of constant renewal more vividly than in the mountains where Moses, Elijah, and George Mallory met

God. To us, the mountains may seem like the most enduring and powerful symbols of all that is implacable and immovable in nature. They are in fact just wrinkles, upfoldings of the plates that form the crust of our earth. They are like baked meringue on a pie, hiding the hot and fluid interior of our globe. Over the last ten billion years the heat of the sun bathing our earth has lost between a quarter and a fifth of its intensity. We have passed through ice ages in which much of the water on this planet was locked up in ice and the mountains played a critical role in the sustaining of life.

For among the minerals and elements trapped in the rock layer was uranium. As it broke down, it emitted vast quantities of energy equivalent to a quarter of a million medium-size nuclear bombs. Trapped in the earth's crust, this heat melted great quantities of iron, one of the most plentiful metals in the earth. Because of its weight, as the iron melted it trickled down through cracks and faults, accumulating more and more at the center of the earth, to form a semisolid core. On it floated the somewhat lighter elements making up the mantle, and on top the lighter rocks that formed the crust. This solidified into giant slabs called tectonic plates moving according to the currents swirling about the core, transmitted through the mantle. As plates were shunted into one another, some were heaved up into massive folds, giving birth to mountains, while others plunged deep into the mantle.

In such a fashion were mountain ranges like the Himalayas born. Eighty million years ago they were part of a large island sixty-four hundred kilometers south of Asia, near Australia. They began moving at nine meters a century northward until they hit the Asian plate about forty to fifty million years ago. Because both were about equal in density they rose together in a massive uplift, forming the mountain mass we now see. The border between India and Tibet marches along these peaks for about twenty-nine hundred kilometers.

Without such mountains the sort of life we know would not exist on earth. They form huge cleansing machines, the lungs of the earth, heaving nine kilometers into the atmosphere; the snow and ice that condense there extract huge amounts of carbon dioxide from the air. This gas trapped in ice and snow reacts with minerals in the rocks to generate great quantities of silica and silicates, much of which becomes clay. This clay, in its turn, absorbs the salts of iron, ferrous compounds, which are then swept down onto the floodplains of massive rivers such as the Ganges, Indus, Mekong, and Yangtze, making fertile the plains of Southeast Asia.

Iron is the lifeblood of our planet. It preserves the core's heat and plays a major part in creating the magnetic field in the atmosphere. Part of this is the Van Allen belts, an electrically charged zone that shields our planet from high-energy cosmic radiation. Without this barrier this radiation would penetrate our atmosphere causing lethal mutations in the cells of many living creatures. For us humans too, iron is our lifeblood. Though all the iron atoms in our bodies would produce only a small nail if they were all extracted and fused together, they play a vital role in our body chemistry. They form part of a complex molecule called heme, which combines with proteins to form hemoglobin. This extraordinary compound permits human blood to absorb about fifty times the amount of oxygen that water can. It regulates this vital but toxic gas in a stable form that can break down or recombine with great speed, thus providing oxygen to burn fats and sugars, bringing surges of energy just when and where they are vital for our survival. No compound similar to hemoglobin exists in the rest of nature.

As God sustains this planet, constantly re-creating human life through the elaborate dance of mountain, water, iron, and blood, so too, on a vastly greater scale, does God continue to keep the entire cosmos in being.

As we gaze into the night sky through the rim of our own galaxy, the Milky Way, we are stunned by the immensity of the universe. The star nearest to us, Alpha Centauri, is just over four light-years away. When we recall that light travels at 186,000 miles per second, that is an astounding distance. Astronomers tell us that the farthest objects we can detect at the edge of our universe lie about fifteen billion light-years away. They are drawing away from us into unknowable darkness. Not only is our universe still expanding, it is still giving birth to new life. On July 4, 1054, Chinese astronomers noted a brilliant blaze in the part of the sky containing the constellation Taurus, the bull. It was so vivid that it was also recorded by Hopi Indians in what is now New Mexico, half a world away. What they saw was a supernova, the explosion of a huge star scattering energy and matter through neighboring areas of space. As this matter condenses, new stars and planets are born. Massive as this explosion was, it was eclipsed by a hypernova observed early in April 2003. This is the collapse of a giant star fifty to a hundred times larger than our sun. This event happened twelve billion years ago. The energy it released is greater than the output of every single star in the Milky Way combined. A tiny fraction of that energy in the form of light has reached us just now.

In the birth of stars we see two competing forces at work, the centrifugal forces of an exploding star versus the drawing power of gravity, which draws all matter together. If the expansion were any greater, our entire universe would fly apart, careening out into endless space. If gravity were any stronger, all the planets and stars and comets and cosmic dust of our universe would collapse inward to vanish into a tiny speck of matter so dense that no light could escape from it. Scientists have reduced all the forces that operate in the universe down to four, three of which operate within atoms and molecules; only one, gravity, acts at a distance. Compared to the others, it is weaker by thirty-eight orders of magnitude (a ten with thirty-seven zeros following it). Yet the balance between these two competing forces is so precise that scientists have yet to determine the exact rate at which the universe is expanding.

This constant creative power of God provides us with an image of the God that Ignatius presents to us in his *Spiritual Exercises*. God is not only the one who sustains all that is, he is also like the primeval fireball that was the origin of our universe. We can picture him as that immense globe of radiant energy that continues to pour out to the furthest corners of the cosmos, creating space as it expands, making a place for the presence of others, for light, for warmth, and ultimately for life itself. At the same time he is like gravity, the weakest of the forces, yet so all-pervasive, permeating all that is with a love that attracts, draws, and pulls everything back into the center so that nothing can eventually overcome its pull.

Theme 2.
God, My Personal Creator

One of the things we notice about the first creation story in Genesis is that it involves many stages and processes. Darkness comes before light; the two are separated; darkness is needed for light to be recognized for what it is. The first three days describe objects that are fixed, without movement. They are stable, creating a locale, a place to which to return and belong. In contrast, days four to six belong to objects that move and search. These are days of eruption, swarming and settling. The constant search of life for a suitable habitat, a place in which to thrive, is a mark of the love that God has set in motion. Already foreshadowed in this account are the human characteristics that will be highlighted in the second narrative: the need to name (Gn 2:20), to seek a mate (Gn 2:22–23), and to search for one's heart's desire (Gn 2:23). In all this, humans mirror the God who made them.

God's plan for life on earth demanded some choices of exquisite narrowness and precision. The sun's light and warmth that pours onto our planet and makes terrestrial life possible is concentrated in a very narrow wavelength, from 0.3 to 1.5 microns (a micron is a thousandth of a millimeter). When we compare that range to the spectrum of electromagnetic energy that washes throughout the universe, we see how tiny is the window within which we live. At one end of the scale are radio waves, some of which can be as much as a kilometer across, whereas the shortest gamma rays have a wavelength of 10^{-16} microns. Now the amazing fact about the radiant energy that makes up immensely more than 99.9 percent of this spectrum is that it is mainly lethal or profoundly damaging to life. God seems to have located us in a world of deadly possibilities yet manages to draw life in all its richness out of this very precariousness.

We find this sense of wonder at life in Jesus' parable of the lilies of the field (Mt 6:25–34). Self-sown, apparently from nowhere, they could have been browsed by cattle, overgrown by weeds, rooted out for useful crops. Yet somehow they thrive, fixing the onlooker with their startling beauty, all unexpected in this wild place. So too, much of the retreatant's life comes unbidden: ancestors, genetic inheritance, temperament, homeland. When we examine these unalterable allotments of providence, we are astounded by the gifts that have been given; "they neither sow nor reap nor gather into barns, and yet your heavenly Father feeds them" (Mt 6:26). Reflecting on that mysterious loving choice of the Jewish people to be the vehicle of salvation to other nations, Isaiah had expressed that same sense of wonder, "Do not fear, for I have redeemed you; I have called you by name, you are mine" (Is 43:1).

We find that the same dynamic of finding freedom and spontaneity in the heart of what is given and fixed also marks the process of the

Exercises. God's refashioning of each retreatant is part of the same creative process by which he guides the cosmos to its destined end.

Theme 3.
The Desires of the Heart

In the Yahwist creation story (Gn 2:4–3:24) a key aspect is how important it is to have someone with whom to share the delight of the garden. Adam, the first man, is given a helpmate to share his life and labor. God not only provides trees that are attractive and nourishing; he walks and shares friendship there with the first couple. Even their downfall comes from reaching out for something they thought would bring them even greater happiness.

The Ignatian retreat is also an exercise in growing the desires of the heart. Out of his own experience Ignatius became convinced that what God most wants for each person is to foster the growth of the deepest and most authentic desires of the human heart. The Exercises are a way of uncovering these desires, sifting them out from the false and ultimately self-destructive longings that those about us and evil spirits in the world can inculcate within us.

The beginning of such discernment is the discovery and acknowledgment of God's love in the retreatant's life so far. The importance of acknowledgment is that it further fans desire, making the one who seeks ever more open and generous, to the extent of asking God to change her heart when it might be leading her away from the heart's maker. In the *Spiritual Exercises*, Ignatius points to two aids that might help to channel these desires in the right direction.

The first of these aids is prayer. To return to our image of the mountain, prayer is like the water that pours from the skies and tumbles its way down the mountainside in torrents and waterfalls. It purifies and nourishes while washing out the salts (like iron compounds) that will end up carrying life in the bloodstream. The water rushes down until it finds its own level, in a pilgrimage to the sea. It may seem sluggish and turgid as it makes its way across the plains, but in its course it irrigates the land and brings life to the soil. We know that sometimes even great watercourses dry up and fail the parched land; at other times flash floods turn quiet rivers into a destructive spate. Prayer too can dry up or turn to ruinous self-deception. That is why Ignatius insists on the presence of a prayer companion, one who listens to the sound of the waters and knows how to detect the dangerous sound of rocks banging together on the riverbed. The prayer guide helps the one making the Exercises to see with clarity the direction and the force of what is rolling around inside. Prayer is the life-bearing water without which the land dries up and crops die.

Theme 4.
The Uses of Distance

High on the mountainside, Moses was able to make out the Jewish encampment far below. From there he saw how few and fragile the people and their flocks looked in contrast to the baked lands of the Sinai spreading out into the shimmering distance. Open to a new vision, he could hear a God who suggested that all other deities were powerless and dead, and that this handful of people could become a new people with a new worship. He could imagine a different world. The experience of prayer in the Exercises is also one of creating a space for imagination, of going to a far-off place, even when we never leave home.

We tend to write our biases and previous experiences even on the face of nature. A pastor in Detroit whom I met took children from inner-city areas for summer camps in the Rockies. He had to teach them how to touch, swing on, and climb trees. They had no knowledge of their feel, size, or strength. Though they walked past a few stunted and blackened trees in their debris-littered streets, none of them knew the smell or texture of a fir or aspens; all they knew were television images of trees. Because of this their imaginations were stunted and dead. The French philosopher Gaston Bachelard said of the imagination:

> The imagination is a tree. It has the integrative virtues of a tree. It has roots and branches. It lives between the earth and the sky. It lives in the earth and in the wind. The imagined tree imperceptibly becomes the cosmological tree, the tree which epitomized a universe, which makes a universe (La terre et les reveries du repos [N.p.: José Certi, 1948]).

Part of the power of the Exercises is to free the imagination and let it discover images and manifestations of God both in the book of scripture and in the book of nature. To win such freedom, those making the Exercises need to learn to see nature afresh with new eyes and understanding.

Theme 5.
Our Beautiful World: Fragile and Threatened

The first astronauts to see planet earth from space were captivated by its blue-green freshness. Its beauty beguiled them in a way which overturned anything they had deemed possible. The image of this planet against the background of space is a vivid reminder of how partial and blinkered our perspective is. What I see each day is only a shell of what is truly there. For instance, I sit in my house in Auckland and look out across my modern city into the Waitemata Harbor and out to Rangitoto Island. Though cloaked in shrub and greenery, its volcanic profile is unmistakable. I recall that this city sits astride fifty-eight volcanic cones, some of which have erupted in the last thousand years. They will erupt again; seismologists tell us they can give us two weeks' warning. I recall that New Zealand straddles the junction of two tectonic plates, one of them edging northward centimeter by centimeter every year. One day it may split part of this northern island clean away. Not only continental drift, but the thinness of the earth's crust, the shallowness of earth's atmosphere—all of these we barely consider, yet they shape our lives.

It is only rarely that we turn our minds to the immensity of the cosmos in which we dwell and the tininess of men and women in the face of this vastness. We struggle to take in how the very size and age of the universe is necessary to have brought forth intelligent life. That the spacing and frequency of supernovae throughout space is exactly what was needed to sow, the seeds of life—carbon, calcium, phosphorus, and iron—barely crosses our minds. Destruction on a grand scale is the very precondition of life.

When one stands in imagination on the moon and looks at this gleaming green and blue planet, it is possible to see how fragile this beauty is. The films *Deep Impact* and *Armageddon* have alerted us to how easily a comet could wipe out much of the life of this globe. Just two weeks before I wrote this paragraph, an asteroid the size of a football field passed by within the orbit of the moon, unobserved until the last moment. A collision would have destroyed a large city. We now know that ecological disasters can occur in what is just the blink of an eyelid in the scale of cosmic time. Even now scientists in the Antarctic are watching the Ross Ice Shelf with great concern. It is melting quickly, and if it collapsed, this could trigger a melt-off of many of the polar glaciers. The worst-case scenario would see the global ocean level rise eight meters, a disaster for low-lying areas such as Bangladesh, many small Pacific islands, and for great coastal cities such as New York, Cape Town, and Sydney.

This vision of our fragile earthly condition could be a source of great fear. Equally, it can lead to the sort of trust in God that we find in these verses from the Book of Wisdom:

> You can show your great power any time you wish, and no one can stand against it. In your sight the whole world is a grain of sand, barely heavy enough to tip a pair of scales, a drop of dew on the ground in the morning. . . . You love everything that exists; you do not despise anything that you have made. If you had not liked it, you would not have made it in the first place (Wis 11:21–22, 24).

To realize that all is gift, given out of love, and yet that nothing can be taken for granted is the attitude of detachment that Ignatius strives to cultivate in those who make the Exercises. It has nothing to do with fatalism or indifference but everything to do with realism and freedom, and it corresponds precisely to the universe in which we live.

Theme 6.
The Significance of One Life

So much that vitally shapes our lives, whether it be the Van Allen belts, the ozone layer, or gravity, is not visible to us. In fact, most of the time these realities do not enter our consciousness. Becoming aware of this paradox can also be a part of the journey of faith of the Exercises. It helps retreatants to realize the great extent to which faith and the invisible pull of God's love can be shaping our lives all unaware. They begin to perceive how the desires of the heart, sometimes so opaque and unheralded, are like gravity or hemoglobin, on whose hidden operation our very existence depends.

This unexpected parallel also has the power of opening the eyes of those who make the Exercises to another key insight. As they delve into scripture passages about the prophets, the life of Jesus, or the early church, a new world opens up. They are often astounded how the power of active imagination, one of the prayer styles recommended by Ignatius, allows them to become Hosea, or the woman wiping Jesus' feet with her hair, or Peter stepping out of the fishing boat to walk on the Sea of Galilee. They see that salvation history is also their history. Once this stride has been taken, the next step is the insight that sacred history did not start with Mary and Joseph, or Isaiah, or even Adam and Eve. It began with the first flaring forth of the primeval fireball from which all matter and life was born. They discover that our human bodies themselves are living records of sacred history, stardust from the explosion of stars billions of years ago.

This understanding allows contemporary men and women to comprehend in a new light the axiom of medieval theologians that the human body is a microcosm of the macrocosm. We are tiny universes in which the history of the cosmos is played out on a small screen. The trillions of synapses and neurons in our brains impart far more information and direction to the relatively remote galaxies of our fingers and toes than the star clusters of the Crab Nebula are beaming to our solar system. Such thoughts can also help retreatants to consider the moral and spiritual power of one human life. A number of anthropologists have commented on the courage and imagination of the first human who dared to pluck a blazing branch from a lightning strike and rush it back to his cave, to kindle fire. These are the acts that change history. Many a time they are effected by little people whose names appear nowhere in the historical annals. We find the same parable implicit in J. R. R. Tolkein's trilogy *The Lord of the Rings*. While the high wizards ally with dwarves and elves to combat the dark powers of Mordor, it is the bumbling Frodo, the hobbit who, concealed and ignored, carries the ring of power whose destruction at Mount Doom brings down the great empire of Sauron, the evil eye.

Theme 7.
The Mystery of Evil

An issue that confronts everyone making the Exercises is the mystery of suffering and evil. This is no abstraction. It can come down to something as concrete as shouting at God, "If you love me, why do you hurt me so much?" These considerations can arise at any time during the long retreat, but often come to a head at the Principle and Foundation Reflection in the first week and the meditations on Jesus' passion in the third week.

There are no simple answers to this great dilemma, which has troubled theologians and mystics alike. Once again it seems that openness to the personal and cosmic dimensions of suffering and violence can provide complementary vistas. Sometimes directors meet retreatants whose idyllic accounts of family and home simply do not gel with the fragility and fear that have marked a religious brother's painful experiences of ministry or a single woman's long list of tentative and broken relationships. Opening up a painful past is never easy, but it is the only pathway into the love of God lying deep below and within this spring of pain that continually bubbles to the surface. Where personal sin is part of that history, forgiveness can always reach back into the roots of the malaise. When poverty, lack of education, or abuse are sources of such evil, the path to healing can be even longer and more difficult.

This mystery also finds near parallels in the world of nature. It is easy to identify the ecological disasters flowing from human greed and ignorance: the burning of vast tracts of Amazonian rainforest or the clear-cutting of irreplaceable hardwood forests in Malaysia and the Solomon Islands. Few people can accept with equanimity the dark face of nature: bands of chimpanzees that will send members up trees to snatch baby colobus monkeys, to dismember and eat them before their mother's eyes, or wasps that plant their eggs within the living bodies of their prey, eating them from within until they drop. Nature as "red in tooth and claw" is also part of God's design, needing to be seen as part of the good creation.

In the cosmos, too, parallel instances of apparently meaningless destruction are also found. Such are the phenomena of black holes, patches of space from which nothing, not even light, escapes. Instead whole galaxies wind down into their open maw, disappearing perhaps forever. What an analogy for sin: the seemingly meaningless absorption and annihilation of what once was so beautiful.

Some retreatants also find Ignatius's stress on evil spirits and their impact on believers' lives and decisions troublesome. They worry that this preoccupation with evil reflects Ignatius's own warlike spirit and echoes the violent religious wars of his age. What preoccupied Ignatius, however, was something dark and malevolent beyond human comprehension, something purely malignant and destructive. We will attempt to enter into this mystery of iniquity in Week Three of the retreat.

Theme 8.
Creation and the Paschal Mystery

The image of the paschal mystery, Jesus' suffering, death, and rising, has often been used to illustrate and explain the process that retreatants pass through over the course of the Exercises. St. Paul himself spoke of the experience of entering the tomb with Christ, likening it to being submerged, drowning, and then emerging to new life (Rom 6:2–4).

Nature is replete with models that can interpret and make sense of the upheaval of one's life that can accompany the making of the Exercises. A moment ago I used the terrifying power of black holes in space as an analogy for sin. Other astronomers see them more positively as a place where matter is transformed and reshaped, to appear as new galaxies in another universe. Another powerful image for the long retreat is the volcano. Its eruptions, scorching gas, lava, and ashes can devastate whole regions. What is equally true is the fertility that is the end result of their action. For the lava and ash they spill are rich in nutrients: iron, magnesium, and phosphates. When these are absorbed by the returning vegetation they bring great richness and vitality. Crops bloom and flourish.

Rocks, too, despite their hardness and brittleness, are sources of hidden life. As we noted, within them tiny particles of uranium can generate heat within their rocky blanket of insulation. But because they are brittle and porous, rocks also allow many of the precious resources within the mantle to seep up onto the surface. Water, iron, and other elements are extruded to fertilize and enrich the soil.

Theme 9.
Re-creation in the Wilderness

In the Christian spiritual tradition both the desert and the garden have been important symbols of the places where one may meet God. St. Macarius used the image of Christ the farmer, his plough the cross, with which he cultivated the abandoned soul and tore out the weeds of sin. Theologians as diverse as Maximus, John of the Cross, Gerrard Winstanley (the seventeenth-century founder of the Diggers, who believed that land belonged to the whole community), and Roger Crab (the noted doctor, author, and vegetarian who lived a decade after Winstanley) have used the same analogy. Crab, a hermit, spoke of his vision in such imagery: "When I was in my earthly garden a-digging with my spade, I saw forth into the Paradise of God from whence my father Adam was cast forth."

Since the time of Anthony of Egypt, the wilderness has also been a symbol of the place of encounter with God. Nor was this phenomenon limited to the Syrian desert. In the Celtic heritage we find wild places like Iona, or the far-flung islands visited by St. Brendan and St. Kevin, as places where God calls his missionaries and mystics to see him in the wilderness and the wild animals they encounter. Environmentalists talk of the need of modern men and women to go to places that are untouched by technology and consumerism, to find themselves in a new way. This is a frequent experience of those making the thirty-day retreat, as they are without outside contact, without television, radio, or newspapers, and without their daily routine of work and social discourse. In the emptiness their senses and imagination are rekindled; God comes alive in images that are not generated by cathode tubes or computer chips.

In the wilderness sometimes men and women see the face of Jesus and their own face for the first time. It seems as if their world had been like the distorting mirrors that one comes across at amusement parks. Looking in the mirror one sees only a twisted and contorted vision. Looking in the mirror, that is Christ, retreatants begin to see their faces transfigured within his features, like something still coming to birth, something breathtakingly beautiful. Initially, what they see might be like looking into the surface of an old family heirloom, all grimed and blackened. During the retreat, however, the Spirit acts like a powerful but gentle polish. Whereas the surface was at first gritty and cloudy, when the grime is wiped away, the retreatant no longer sees the metal, but rather the spotless image that smiles back in amazement. In the solitude of the Exercises the image of Christ can be rediscovered afresh.

*Week*1*One*

OPENING TO GOD'S GIFTS

I have suggested that setting out on the Exercises is somewhat akin to an adventure. Like those who climb Mt. Everest, we may discover that this adventure will be a life-transforming experience. Just as the view from the summit of Everest is like nothing else on earth, so too will the new perspective we gain through our ascent be unique for us. While the retreat may not pose physical challenges, it may be challenging in a different way. The hardest work for us may come when we return to our familiar surroundings and try to live out of this new vision of ourselves and the world that we have discovered.

Perhaps an apt image of this challenge is one that was familiar to the aboriginal people who wandered through the vast unmapped desert plains of the Australian interior. They believed that the whole land had been sung into existence by their first ancestors, who laid down melody lines that traversed the continent. Each rocky spur or billabong had its own song and story, unique and unchanging. When they traveled in their small bands, they had no maps or compasses but followed the melodies that stretched from horizon to horizon. In so doing, they believed that they were creating their world anew, making their children a part of the land and setting their story in it. In making the Exercises, each retreatant is likewise walking a well-trodden path, previously set down by Ignatius and the first Jesuits. That journey, as we will see, is in itself an attempt to reenact the life story of Jesus Christ.

Each attempt to do so will be a new interpretation, a new sketch, and a new understanding. This in turn may modify the self-understanding and lives of many other people.

Continuing with the metaphor of the journey, we may say that Week One of the Exercises is like a large-scale topographical map. It situates us on our journey and roughly sets out the various stages. You learn how to read the map and cover the ground, and how to cope with some of the hazards of cross-country trekking. Someone who successfully traverses the journey of the first week is then ready to take on the more detailed and intricate gorges and ascents of Weeks Two to Four.

Underlying the Exercises are four foundational faith convictions:

- I must accept I am only a creature, not God.
- Yet I have been freely invited by God to be his friend and co-creator of the world.
- I confess that at times I have tried to act like God or at other times to deny my godliness.
- When I genuinely desire freedom and know that God wants me to have this gift, then God will give me the strength and show me the path to attain it.

The work of the first week of the Exercises is to accept these principles as the road map by which I will plot out my life. In the next three weeks retreatants see in detail what this will mean for their particular life situation. We will look briefly at each of these four key principles.

The acknowledgment "I am a creature" is the starting point of honesty for us. It leaves us open to a sense of wonder, that we will always be able to discover more and more about ourselves and the processes of creation and to never say the last word. It leaves us free to be imperfect, unfinished, with lots of carving, shaping, and polishing still to be done. Owning our place as creatures also puts us as humans in solidarity with all other creatures on this planet, be they earthworms or grizzly bears, bindweeds or sequoias. We cannot ignore or disclaim our identity and accountability as children of the earth.

No other creature is ever tempted to behave as if it were God. A story from the life of the famous rabbi Moses de Léon illustrates why humankind is so open to this temptation. It is based on that mysterious incident in Gn 28:10–17 when Jacob dreams of a ladder going up to heaven. Most translations of verse 16 of this passage read, "God was in this place and I did not know." But one of the Jewish texts repeats the first "I" to read, "God was in this place and I, I did not know." The scribe takes the first "I" *(Anochi)* to be a revelation of a new name for God. Human words and divine words never have exactly the same meaning, because of the infinite distance between God and humankind. Yet this is not true of the first person singular (I). What makes each person unique is that when he or she recognizes something in the world and is aware of this recognition, each knows that, despite seeing this thing differently from God and other individuals, they are sharing the same experience of self-awareness that God has. In this lies a certain godliness. The work of the first week is coming to the insight that at the heart of creation is God's love and care for the world. Like Jacob, each of us is called to recognize and share in that. That is what matters, and my smallness and sinfulness is little by comparison.

The second principle tells us that, while we are creatures, we are in a certain sense very special creatures. Being aware as God is, we cannot evade a sense of being subjects operating in this world. This gives us a responsibility for the world that we cannot ignore. This is the context for the penetration of the mystery of sinfulness that is central to the first week of the Exercises, the area covered in the third principle. We cannot stand outside creation and the consequences of our actions within it. That is the first context of sin. Sin is turning in on oneself; it leads to a growing inability to perceive the reality and needs of others. The revivalist and mystic Jonathan Edwards captures this superbly when he speaks of the original sin that distorted human vision:

> Immediately upon the fall, the mind of man shrank from its primitive greatness and expandedness, to an exceeding smallness and contractedness. Before, his soul was under the government of that noble principle of divine love, whereby it was enlarged to the comprehension of all his fellow-creatures and their welfare. [After the fall] ... all this excellent enlargedness of man's soul

was gone, and henceforth he himself shrank, as it were into a little space, circumscribed and closely shut up within itself, to the exclusion of all things else. Sin, like some powerful astringent, contracted his soul to the very dimension of selfishness; and God was forsaken and fellow-creatures forsaken, and man retired within himself, and became totally governed by narrow and selfish principles and feelings.

For other people, sin has a different face, that of self-diminishment. Such people see themselves as failures, as having no worth except through their work or relationships, or to the extent that they serve others. Abused children and battered wives often suffer in this way. But because none of us was raised in a perfect family, there will be some residue of self-rejection and anger in the best and strongest of retreatants. Dealing with this legacy of family wounds is a frequent part of the work of the first week. The Exercises are not a form of psychotherapy and were not designed as such. Yet to the extent that they touch the same roots of rejection, buried resentment, and self-hatred that is the stuff of analysis, they inevitably will work toward the restoration of healthy relationships, though through very different dynamics. One of the fruits of the first week is to come to see sin not in legal terms, but as the marring and distortion of relationship. Such relationships will be seen broadly, including our relationship with God as well as our relationships with other people, ourselves, and creation.

The other deep conviction that underlies the first week is that God longs for our freedom. To come to that sense of freedom often involves paradox. Sometimes, like addicts, we have to admit we cannot break free by our own efforts. We have to admit that we are not coping in a particular job or relationship and we need to reach out for help, both from God and from others, perhaps friends or professionals. Having done that, there is often a great sense of relief; we can let go of façades and pretences and accept the astounding good news that God loves us with total acceptance. Out of this grows a deep sense of gratitude for so much in our lives. Realizing that preoccupation with our own faults and sins can end in despair, and entering deeply into the first week, we come instead to rely on the limitless compassion and mercy of God.

This experience of conversion is marked by a change in the image of God. Images of God as bookkeeper or disciplinarian give way to the image of God as a father who carries his child on his back or a mother comforting a crying infant at her breast. In many ways it is the transformation of imagination that is the deepest work accomplished in this first week, a whole new way of seeing one's life, as is beautifully caught by Robert Banks in his book *God the Worker* on the images of God:

> Conversion, therefore, requires more than a change of mind, heart or will. It requires a change of imagination also. It is not just scientific revolutions that require a 'paradigm shift' or shift in basic pattern of understanding, but personal revolutions as well. Logical arguments, emotional appeals, stirring challenges are not enough. The collage of images which fill our minds—from well-developed world views to fragmentary and even contradictory images of reality—must undergo some change. It is only images that can drive out other images. It is only authentic images of God that can overturn inauthentic ones.

Day 1
Searching for the God Who Loves Me

Prayer Desire

I ask for my heart to be open to the hidden God who longs to disclose himself to me.

Ignatian Focus

I turn all my internal senses—memory, understanding, free will, and imagination—upon the meditation proposed, whether it is a biblical scene or a point suggested by Ignatius. (*The Spiritual Exercises* 45)

Introduction

Each of us longs to be free, simply to have some space to shape our own life and destiny. St. Ignatius sees the fulfillment of this desire as one of the fruits of entering into the first week of *The Spiritual Exercises* without reservation. This longing for freedom grows within us on the journey that we are now beginning. It wells up within us as we come to the deep conviction that God also longs for us to enjoy such freedom. This may be a giant stride, for it may involve not just a new understanding of God, but sometimes a totally new way of seeing and accepting ourselves and what has brought us to this place.

To make such a journey is to walk with Wisdom as she is portrayed in the Hebrew scriptures. She is a companion who shows us how to savor from the heart and not just to know abstractly: "For you love all things that exist, and detest none of the things that you have made" (Wis 11:24). When Wisdom speaks, it is through images of the seasons, stars, light, and precious jewels, things that delight the senses. So too does Ignatius insist on the role of active imagination, which is, as it were, a handmaiden of Wisdom, when he suggests that retreatants turn all their senses, internal and external, on the meditation that he proposes.

In this way Ignatius draws all the faculties into harmony, unleashing the power of the symbols of nature to touch every level of the retreatant's being. Because we are multilevel creatures—body, soul, and spirit—we can be sold into slavery through the failure of any one of these levels. Equally too, Lady Wisdom, dressed in the humble attire of the imagination, can sneak within the citadel of our being and cast off our shackles before the watchers at the gate who never sleep know that she has gained entrance. Many of the discoveries of modern physics and science also have the same capacity: the ability to open us up to a grander and deeper vision of God.

Ecological Reflection

When Einstein arrived at his famous equation $e=mc^2$ he opened up the possibility of seeing the universe with new eyes. He gave us a new wisdom. What his equation showed us is that everything that seems solid and indivisible is made of tiny particles, each of which can be converted into vast amounts of energy. He taught us to see matter as frozen energy, that in a walnut, or a book, or in a human finger there is stored enough energy to light a city, blast open a mountain, or dry up a small lake. Everything we see is frozen energy, boundless potential.

Similarly, all we see is held together by four different forces. Three of these are locked deep within the atom, and mostly we are unaware of their existence. The fourth of these, gravity, is the weakest yet the one of which we are aware. The reach of gravity is so pervasive and total that the fate of our universe lies in its hands. Against all the forces of repulsion and the outward thrust that are the legacy of the birth of our universe, gravity holds and restrains. It is an omnipresent power of attraction, drawing all back to the center to the maternal womb of creation. It is an invisible dynamism, almost imperceptible at the small and local level, yet holding all in balance. It is an image of God's love, invisible, almost undetectable, the cement that holds all that is, in being.

Wisdom teaches us to see and taste this love everywhere. Once we attain this vision, our sense of the meaning of all around us is changed. There is a new freedom in all we behold. In this first week of the Exercises, Ignatius invites us to identify and let go of all that stops us from reaching out and embracing this wisdom. In the following passage from the prophet Isaiah we see how he was also able to see the wisdom and mercy of God imaged in the rain and snow that fell about him. If our eyes are to be opened in a similar way, the first step toward this is to desire it and ask it of God.

Scripture Reflection: Is 55:6–13

Seek the Lord while he is to be found, call upon him while he is near. . . . Let them return to the Lord, that he may have mercy on them, and to our God, for he will abundantly pardon. . . . For as the heavens are higher than the earth, so are my ways higher than your ways and my thoughts than your thoughts. For as the rain and the snow come down from heaven, and do not return there until they have watered the earth, making it bring forth and sprout, giving seed to the sower and bread to the eater, so shall my word be that goes out from my mouth; it shall not return to me empty, but it shall accomplish that which I purpose, and succeed in the thing for which I sent it. . . . The mountains and the hills before you shall burst into song, and all the trees of the field shall clap their hands.

Scripture Commentary

To the Jews who lived as exiles in Babylon six centuries before the coming of Christ, it must have seemed that they were just the plaything of other great powers. Once courted by the throne of Babylon, then conquered, plundered, and taken off into exile, they could now see the pendulum swinging toward a resurgent Persian empire. In the so-called Book of Consolation the prophet Isaiah assures the people that it is the pagan empires that are instead the instruments of God. The great Persian general Cyrus would serve as God's anointed to restore the Jews to their land once again. All the failings and sins of the Jewish people would be forgotten, for Yahweh would be faithful to his word of restoration. That word would not only change history; it would also reverse the suffering of the people, the hard labor, the stubborn desert, and the malicious thorns that were God's punishment for human disobedience. Even the desert and the meager Syrian vegetation would be transformed as God led his people back to their own home, where they would see his glory once more after he had hidden his face from them.

This word can be equally powerful today for our personal situation.

Additional Passages

Lk 11:5–11   We beg for God's door to be opened to us.

Dt 1:29–32   In all our personal history God has been carrying us on life's journey.

Questions for Reflection

1. Do I see myself as basically free, or is my life hedged in by restraints and fears? Can I name them and lay them before God?
2. In what ways does the physical world around me speak to me of the God hidden within it?
3. Are there places, experiences, people that act for me as keyholes to the divine, allowing me a glimpse of the God who loves me?

A Final Thought

The Bible is one piece of enduring literature that was not written by the conquering class, but rather by the losers. Ninety-five percent of the Bible was written by people who were oppressed or occupied or enslaved or poor. That's extraordinary. That kind of literature doesn't last; it never even gets written. And that's what makes the Bible an extraordinary book.

—Richard Rohr

Day 2
Hearing God's Hidden Word

Prayer Desire

I thank and praise God for his generosity manifest in the world and ask that I may see it with fresh eyes.

Ignatian Focus

I thank God for all the good things I have received. (*The Spiritual Exercises* 43)

Introduction

At the top of the South Island of New Zealand lie the Marlborough Sounds, an extensive network of drowned valleys invaded by the sea. Perhaps the first Europeans to visit this area were the members of the British expedition of James Cook in January 1770. A young naturalist on the ship, Joseph Banks, relates how he was awakened by a deafening dawn chorus of birds singing from the mainland, predominant among which were the ringing sound of myriad bellbirds. One can no longer hear such astounding dawn choruses. Ironically, one of the reasons for this is probably the arrival of Norwegian rats, stowaways on Cook's ship, *Endeavour,* that took the opportunity to head for the richer food supplies on shore. This voracious predator soon eclipsed the inroads of the Polynesian rat, *kiore,* into the native bird population.

New Zealand was unique in its isolation; no large animals and virtually no mammals had arrived there. Birds of every conceivable size and variety filled the lowland forests and stands of mountain beech. There were 164 species, many flightless. Among the latter were a dozen species of moa, some up to two meters tall. Swooping through the trees was also Haast's eagle, the largest in the world. Most of these native species have now disappeared forever. Some were hunted to extinction; many dwellers on the forest floor fell prey to rats, stoats, and ferrets. Others vanished because the native trees of the river forests in which they roosted and fed—the *kauri, kahikatea, puketea, rata, matai,* and *maire*— were felled for ships' spars or to create farmland for settlers.

Ecological Reflection

We who live on these far-flung islands will never see the native forests that once cloaked our land from the rim of the Pacific to halfway up the Southern Alps, nor the bird life that thronged the canopy of our forests just a millennium ago. The very awareness of what we have lost irreparably is a reminder to us of the almost prodigal character of God and of nature. Sore as this loss has been, it is important to remember that the first settlers that came here believed they were creating a better life for themselves and their children. Many of the Europeans who came were fleeing from the crofter clearances of Scotland or the potato famine in Ireland. Others came to escape the rigid class and political systems of nineteenth-century England. As colonists have so often done, they imposed their needs and prejudices on the land, ignoring the detailed knowledge of the local people of this unique place, and so destroyed many of the fragile links in the network, holding birds, trees, and people in mutual dependence in Aotearoa-New Zealand.

We may believe that, if we had the same chances, we might have prevented or at least lessened the colossal loss of fauna and flora. Yet in many ways it was only the loss that opened our eyes to the uniqueness of what we had. It requires new eyes to see new possibilities. As we begin the second day of our journey with God, we deepen our realization that becoming open to a new future is often inextricably mixed with coming to realize how much we were blind to what we did in the past. Jesus too used the beauty of the world around him to remind his followers just how complacent and ungrateful they could be.

Scripture Reflection: Lk 12:22–31

He said to his disciples, "Therefore I tell you, do not worry about your life, what you will eat, or about your about body, what you will wear. For life is more than food, and the body more than clothing. Consider the ravens: they neither sow nor reap, they have neither storehouse nor barn, and yet God feeds them. Of how much more value are you than the birds! And can any of you by worrying add a single hour to your span of life? If then you are not able to do so small a thing as that, why do you worry about the rest? Consider the lilies, how they grow: they neither toil nor spin; yet I tell you, even Solomon in all his glory was not clothed like one of these. But if God so clothes the grass of the field, which is alive today and tomorrow is thrown into the oven, how much more will he clothe you—you of little faith! And do not keep striving for what you are to eat and what you are to drink, and do not keep worrying. For it is the nations of the world that strive after all these things, and your Father knows that you need them. Instead, strive for his kingdom, and these things will be given to you as well.

Scripture Commentary

Of all the evangelists, Luke is most preoccupied with the suffering and marginalized of the world. His parables are full, of cheated widows, lost items, and lost people. He specially focuses on those who believe that many possessions (the parable of the rich landowner), priestly status (the parable of the good Samaritan), or self-righteousness (the parable of the Pharisee and the publican) are going to give them a special say with God. Though God gives his Spirit to the poor among the Jews (Anna, Mary, Simeon), he will also pour this out on aliens (the Roman centurion, the Ethiopian eunuch). In this passage Luke is asking the reader to ponder on what brings security and true happiness in life, and whether intense worry about food, clothes, or status can give us any guarantees. The examples he chooses, ravens and lilies, further highlight his message. Ravens are scavengers and were despised by the Jews; lilies, though beautiful, are so ephemeral. Both underline the shortness and fragility of life, even human life. Yet one detects Jesus' love and compassion even for them, and we too experience sadness for so many lost species and the beauty they once embodied.

Additional Passages

Rv 3:20	I am standing at the door knocking.
Ps 95:1–9	Let us listen to God and acclaim him.

Questions for Reflection

1. With what sort of eyes do I view the world around me: as pragmatist, farmer, scientist, poet?
2. Do I ever reflect on the fleeting and fragile nature of human life?
3. Are such reflections a source of wonder or worry for me? Why?

A Final Thought

This morn I was awakd by the singing of the birds ashore from whence we are distant not a quarter of a mile, the numbers of them were certainly very great who seemd to strain their throats with emulation perhaps; their voices were certainly the most melodious wild musick I have ever heard, almost imitating small bells but with the most tuneable silver sound imaginable to which maybe the distance was no small addition. On enquiring of our people I was told that they had observd them ever since we have been here, and that they begin to sing at about 1 or 2 in the morn and continue until sunrise, after which they are silent all day like our nightingales.

—Sir Joseph Banks

Day 3
Seeing the Truth of God

Prayer Desire

I pray to be so free in looking on the beauty and greatness of God that I can entrust myself unreservedly into his hands.

Ignatian Focus

One of the values of each living creature on the face of this planet is that it can serve to help humans to come to see the purpose for which they were created. (*The Spiritual Exercises* 23)

Introduction

Late in January of 1991, I flew out of Nauru, an island in the central Pacific Ocean sitting almost atop the equator. As the packed 737 climbed steeply over the coral reef that lay just off the edge of the airstrip, we banked and flew over the twenty-one square kilometers that make up the island. For the first time I gained a panoramic view of where I had lived and worked for the past five weeks, on this isolated atoll. During my stay I had visited the phosphate diggings on the central plateau three times. The dirt road leading to the diggings soon emerges from dusty and stunted shrubs onto a pockmarked plain. Pitting begins on each side: clumps of coral knobs stretch like exposed reefs parallel to the road. After a mile or two the route resembles a flyover. All around and below, columns of coral, exposed when the phosphate was dynamited and scooped out, stand like pinnacles, some up to twenty meters high. The blaring tropical sun creates dark hollows and steeples of light stretching out to every horizon.

On first visit this seemed just a part of the island—its economic base. Wheeling above the island, however, I saw it all from a new perspective. The central plateau dominated the picture. Its bald and ravaged skull made up 80 percent of the land. The fringe of green that ringed the atoll was just a narrow band between sea and earth. Yet when I lived on the coastal road that runs around Nauru, it seemed that the houses, shops, and schools clustered there were the island. How different it looked from the air.

Every island and every life can be viewed from multiple vantage points. In the end, only God's total view can encompass the partial truth of each of these visions.

Ecological Reflection

The island of Nauru grew wealthy by exporting its bedrock. For the first half of the twentieth century this had been for the profit of its colonial masters: England, Australia, and New Zealand. After Nauru took over control of the Phosphate Commission in 1970, the pace of exploitation did not slow down but speeded up. For twenty giddy years Nauru was the richest island nation (on a per capita basis) in the Pacific. When I was there, some of the costs were beginning to show. The average age of mortality was low (early fifties). Many died of obesity-related diseases such as diabetes. There was very little work to do, so people watched endless videos in their houses. With no need to grow food or make handicrafts, everything needed came by ship from Australia. Now that the phosphate has run out and many of its investments have not brought great returns, the island nation faces once more the humiliating prospect of becoming a welfare client of Australia.

This tension between appearance and reality touches many aspects of nature. A good instance of this is the ambiguity that we humans feel toward radioactive elements such as uranium. We know now that the uranium that vaporized entire sections of the cities of Hiroshima and Nagasaki was no larger than a cricket ball or baseball. Just a very small proportion of the matter within the uranium was transformed to pure energy—but enough to devastate a city. As mentioned earlier many tons of uranium solidified in rocks within the earth as it cooled. Its gradual breakdown caused enough heat to melt iron ores that trickled down through the fissures and rents of the crust to make their way down to form a semiliquid core. Though it lies beneath our feet, we are usually totally unaware that it is essential to all life on earth. For this pool of molten iron led to the planet separating out into three distinct zones: core, mantle, and crust. The rocks that solidified in the crust are the fabric out of which life was made. When Ice Ages gripped the planet in cold so intense that a third of the land was shrouded in ice and three-quarters of the water locked up in glaciers, the furnace hidden in the core continued to pour out the lava that would be the seedbed of new life. As we go about our daily lives, we hardly give a thought to this underground furnace, essential to our survival as a planet and as a species. How well it illustrates the tenuousness of human survival—that the same energy that sustains our planet's body heat could also vaporize us, flesh and blood.

When as a species we are so blind to the elemental forces on which our very existence depends, it is hardly surprising that we can be wildly askew as to what will bring us personal happiness and fulfillment. One does not have to be much of a cynic to look at full-page spreads in Hollywood magazines on the latest celebrity marriage, each swearing perpetual happiness and joy, to ask how many years, or even months, this ecstasy of self-deceit will last before divorce sets in. Perhaps that is why we are so fearful and slow to believe in a God who wants our happiness and freedom immensely more than we do. Despite our protestations of trust, we are typically fearful to let go and admit that God can shape and lead our lives to deeper satisfaction than our own unaided striving can achieve. That is why early in the first week of the retreat, Ignatius proposes to all his retreatants the exercise that he called "the Principle and Foundation." It is an invitation to surrender our plans for our lives in favor of God's plan for my life. The Book of Wisdom likewise invites us to reflect that it is God's love and wisdom that sustains all creation in existence.

Scripture Reflection: Wis 11:21–12:1

For it is always in your power to show great strength, and who can withstand the might of your arm? Because the whole world before you is like a speck that tips the scales, and like a drop of morning dew that falls on the ground. But you are merciful to all, for you can do all things, and you overlook people's sins, so that they may repent. For you love all things that exist, and detest none of the things that you have made, for you would not have made anything if you hated it. How would anything have endured if you had not willed it? Or how would anything not called forth by you have been preserved? You spare all things, for they are yours, O Lord, you who love the living. For your immortal spirit is in all things.

Scripture Commentary

Wisdom is one of the last books of the Old Testament, written perhaps just a hundred years before Jesus. Its purpose was to encourage Jews living in an environment utterly steeped in Greek philosophy and values, possibly the great Egyptian city of Alexandria. There Jews were despised as backward and ignorant. The writer of Wisdom actually uses many Greek ideas to try to demonstrate how Jewish religion not only includes but far exceeds the religious and moral vision of the Greek world. He offers a new vision of the creation and Jewish history to show how it goes far beyond and is much deeper than anything that the best of Greek thought can offer.

Additional Passages

Jn 4:7–10   Jesus promises the gift of living water, a symbol of eternal wisdom.

Jb 38:39—39:30   God provides for the earth and all its creatures.

Questions for Reflection

1. Am I aware how profoundly my life and the life of all I love is rooted in the earth on which I stand?
2. Does it ever occur to me that the food I eat is a partaking in the body of the earth given in love for me by God?
3. Do I ever give thanks for the gifts of warmth and water? Of earth and its fruitfulness?

A Final Thought

The Principle and Foundation is a nonscriptural meditation proposed by Ignatius at this stage in the first week. Joseph Tetlow has rewritten this text in simple words and ideas. I have used his framework but rewritten it fairly extensively to locate it in a cosmic setting with a global ethic.

Every part of the universe is shaped so as to achieve God's ultimate plan by praising, revering, and living according to God's will. Human beings have a unique role in this cosmic vision.

All things on the face of and under the earth come within the companionship and stewardship of humankind as part of God's intention to harmonize God's creation in Christ.

In using the goods of creation, therefore, divine harmony comes about when humans use these gifts to fulfill their deepest call in Christ and resolutely turn away from anything that could deflect them from that calling.

Concretely, unless we have some higher moral duty, such as to our children, we should avoid getting tied down to any particular created object. We should strive to remain totally in balance before all the good gifts of creation. Before making any decision, we should avoid getting locked into categories such as "I will do only things that safeguard my health and avoid anything that could make me ill," or "I will always strive to be wealthy rather than poor," or "to live a longer rather than a shorter life." By opting for such a strategy, we can live in harmony when we need to make choices about our use of God's creatures.

We commit ourselves to live in total harmony, choosing solely on the basis of what will help us to achieve the sort of destiny for which God originally brought forth all of creation.

—Joseph Tetlow

Day 4
Knowing God's Love as the Basis of All That Is Good

Prayer Desire
I pray to be free of the illusion that I can control my world or my life by my own efforts.

Ignatian Focus
When I reflect in a more mature way, I see that God is in every creature according to his own essence, presence, and power. So every creature is good, regardless how trivial or useless it seems to me. (*The Spiritual Exercises* 39)

45

Introduction

When we go back to where we were born, we are sometimes shocked by new apartments, shops, old identities dead and gone, yet the land, the shape of hills, rivers, and plains is still familiar. If it were possible to see back millions of years ago, we would be more shocked for even the mountains and great rivers might not be there. A younger and more savage land might be thousands of miles from where it now lies. For each of the continents is slowly sliding on vast plates riding the heat surges that make the mantle of our earth arch and buckle over the millennia.

In a somewhat similar way each of us is a tiny continent, our foundations sunk deep within the planet and its history, our origins hidden deep below. We float on the back of our ancestors and the land in which they lived. Like continents, we too bear the scars of divides and rifts, places where two plates far underground have collided. Mountains have been heaved up and synclines pushed into the sea along such faults. They are regions of volcanoes and earthquakes. Each of us bears fault lines, a record of the tensions and pressure points of our lives, not just personal but issues of temperament, health, and genetic weaknesses that go far back into our lineage. Sin too is part of this endowment.

Though such fault lines are testaments to personal weakness, they are also the great bearers of life. Where fault lines and volcanoes occur so too does earth's heat and inner wealth reach the surface. After the eruption and the violence, the cooling lava is the source of great fertility. It brings trace elements as well as silicates and phosphates that are vital for rich new soil. Around the mountains grow the plains rich with new life and growth.

Ecological Reflection

This scientific vision of the shaping of lands out of the wanderings and collisions of great continental plates gives us a sobering vision of our earth's history: a remorseless and violent process over which humans have little control. We know, however, that human actions can speed up or slow down these dynamics. We see this in current phenomena such as global warming or the hole in the ozone layer. Most scientists agree that human contributions to pollution, the clear-cutting of tropical rainforests, and higher levels of carbofluorides and carbon dioxide are part of such problems. Human greed and exploitation is without doubt a major contributor to such behaviors. But at the same time it is the complexity of the global economic system that drives such systems. Many people look at the runaway character of global trade and politics, shrug their shoulders, and say it is beyond their abilities to understand, let alone change.

Freedom comes when I acknowledge that no single individual can control the movement of the continents, nor can anyone shift the intricate overlay of social and economic culture that humans have patterned upon this planet. Yet what I can do is to take responsibility for the foibles of the tiny continent that I am, its mountains, fault lines, and plains. I can encourage or ravage their fertility, making them a source of life or slow death. This is in my hands. In a similar way the prophet Isaiah urges the Jewish people not to fear, for the same God who originally called them to be his people will also lead them out of the slavery of Babylon, no matter how unconquerable the barriers seem.

Scripture Reflection: Is 43:1–8

But now thus says the LORD, he who created you, O Jacob, he who formed you, O Israel: Do not fear for I have redeemed you; I have called you by name, you are mine. When you pass through the waters, I will be with you; and through the rivers, they shall not overwhelm you; when you walk through fire you shall not be burned, and the flame shall not consume you. . . . Because you are precious in my sight, and honored, and I love you, I give people in return for you, nations in exchange for your life. Do not fear, for I am with you; I will bring your offspring from the east, and from the west I will gather you; I will say to the north, "Give them up," and to the south, "Do not withhold; bring my sons and my daughters from the end of the earth—everyone who is called by my name, whom I created for my glory, whom I formed and made. Bring forth the people who are blind, yet have eyes, who are deaf, yet have ears!

Scripture Commentary

For the Jews who have been exiled for two generations in Babylon, God promises were something astonishing. Their rescue from slavery will be so overwhelming an experience of new life that the writer can use no other terms than the language that the first writer in Genesis used to record God's creation of the world. This restoration from exile is a pledge of immense love, for other greater and more powerful gentile nations will not experience this sign of favor. God will do this for Israel because Yahweh names himself as the nation's kin, a term very rarely used of God in the Hebrew Bible, for it is built on bonds of blood and clan obligations. The waters and rivers that seem great barriers to the journey of the Chosen People will be in no way impassible, because God achieves the impossible for those he has chosen in love. The concluding verses point to an immense gathering of scattered peoples—something global, exceeding human dreams. God's love is not provincial. Though it begins from Israel as a privileged people, it flows out irresistibly to the whole world.

Additional Passages

1 Sm 3:1–10   The call of Samuel.

Eph 3:14–21   The power of completion given through Christ.

Questions for Reflection

1. What are the eruptions and fault lines in my life? Am I capable of mapping them, or do I need the help of family and professionals in achieving this?
2. Do these fault lines go deep within my family and ethnic lineage? Can I see them in my siblings and wider family?
3. What life and richness have these volcanic zones contributed to me as a person?

A Final Thought

Today the Hidden One is manifested, and the Unseen One is seen, that he may make us seers.

Today the Unhumbled humbly inclines his head to his own servant, that he may free us from servitude.

Today he humbles the hills unto servitude and makes the rivers as
the sea. All that nature of the waters is blessed and hallowed.
Today come the currents of grace of the Holy Spirit, and all
creatures are inundated therewith.
Today the briny waters of the sea are changed to sweetness at the
appearing of God.
Today all creatures appear clad in splendor at the appearing of God.
Today the waters appear above for the salvation of the world.
Today the garden appears, let us rejoice in righteousness unto
eternal life.
Today the earth trembling, but joyfully, receives the Creator's foot
steps upon it.
Today the sins and transgressions of the race of Adam are blotted
out in the water of Jordan, and the earth's face is renewed at
the appearing of God.
Today the shut and barred gate of the garden is opened to
mankind.

—Armenian Prayer for Epiphany

Day 5
Acknowledging Sin in Cosmic History

Prayer Desire

I beg God, even to the point of tears, to see and accept my com-
plicity with sin in this world.

Ignatian Focus

I reflect on the sin of angels: that exquisite beings, once beautiful
and intelligent, rebelled and were transformed from creatures of
grace to embodiments of malice. (*The Spiritual Exercises* 50)

Introduction

Late one winter I was hiking with some university students in the Hollyford Valley in Fiordland. It is the most mountainous region of New Zealand, famed for its jagged ranges, intensely green and forested river valleys, and frequent torrential downpours. We were staying in a cabin in the motor camp. I walked across the camp to use the bathroom facilities and was ambushed by the night sky. No light save the stars reached there, hundreds of kilometers from the nearest large city. In that inky darkness the constellations blazed with fierce intensity, the carpet of the sky right across the valley festooned with spiral nebulae, clumpy constellations, individual jewel-like stars, and liberal dustings of galaxies so distant they were like flour scattered on the rolling board of the heavens. Our beautiful earth seems a complex and unique home. As we look out through the Milky Way, we are peering through the million, million stars of our galaxy; and this is just one of the more than a billion galaxies we know of in the universe.

In this immensity we seem very tiny and insignificant. Until a few centuries ago most of the peoples of earth believed that the cosmos was inhabited by other intelligent beings. While the beauty of the earth convinced them that some of these beings were good, they believed that there were powerful evil influences holding sway in the cosmos as well. Today, with our scientific and rational mentality, we may be prone to dismiss this notion. Yet this would seem to be an arrogant assumption.

A new perspective on this enigma comes to us from Celtic spirituality, one of the early strands of our Catholic heritage. Even in the most isolated mountain in Kerry the shepherd never felt alone. All about he felt other spirit worlds: the fairies, elemental presences, departed spirits of loved ones, and angelic and guardian spirits. Part of the continuing success of Tolkien's *Lord of the Rings* trilogy, in both novel and film form, has been for many people a rediscovery of the spectrum of life that many primitive peoples have intuited. We never have been home alone in the universe. The Bible and St. Ignatius both show deep awareness that we are part of far wider cosmic struggles. Tolkien depicts Saruman (once called the White) chopping down his forests to turn his lands into a vast and ugly arsenal once he had turned his eyes toward and fallen under the sway of the Lord of the Dark Tower. The destruction of beauty in the pursuit of power is still one of the marks of the presence of the demonic in our world.

Ecological Reflection

One of the most frequent analogies for sin in the Bible is blindness. The kingdom of dark against the kingdom of light is one of the central themes in the gospel of John. Blindness can happen through accident or mutilation. More often it is the result of a slow degeneration of the muscles of the lens or a creeping disease like cataracts. It is a most apt image of sin, for over and over we see instances of human unwillingness to look at the evidence when something terrible is occurring. José Saramago's novel *Blindness* captures this tendency with chilling accuracy as various officials first try to deny the signs of an epidemic, then isolate and attempt to hide the sufferers, until order totally collapses. Sometime the blind see again; most often they do not.

There have always been poverty, squalor, and some environmental destruction where large groups of humans have lived together. The difference in today's world is that we have the medical and scientific knowledge, the resources and the technology for much of this to be eliminated. In our liberal tradition various thinkers have proposed some factor such as overpopulation, capitalism, or government over-regulation, new technology or the lack of technology as the critical factor that has blocked the coming of an ecologically responsible and integrated world.

Few scholars are brave enough to name evil as part of the world's pollution. Even when they do acknowledge personal moral failures and their impact on society, few are willing to see these personal failings as counterpoint to the struggles of power and principalities that are much wider than our earthly home. This vision was central to the worldview of Jesus and Paul; it was assumed in much that Ignatius proposes. Our refined knowledge of psychology and sociology can help us understand and explain the dynamics of the psychic roots and contagion of human evil, but it cannot account for the hatred of goodness and delight in the dark and twisted that is so endemic in human history. Often we have to pray for our eyes to be open to this truth. The blind beggar outside Jericho offers us a clear example of the sort of tenacity called for in this.

Scripture Reflection: Mk 10:46–52

They came to Jericho. As he and his disciples and a large crowd were leaving Jericho, Bartimaeus son of Timaeus, a blind beggar, was sitting by the roadside. When he heard that it was Jesus of Nazareth, he began to shout out and say, "Jesus, son of David, have mercy on me!" Many sternly ordered him to be quiet, but he cried out even more loudly, "Son of David, have mercy on me!" Jesus stood still and said, "Call him here." And they called the blind man, saying to him, "Take heart; get up, he is calling you." So throwing off his cloak, he sprang up and came to Jesus. Then Jesus said to him, "What do you want me to do for you?" The blind man said, "My teacher, let me see again." Jesus said to him, "Go; your faith has made you well." Immediately he regained his sight and followed him on the way.

Scripture Commentary

Of all the gospels it is Mark that most emphasizes the many levels of conflict that Jesus has to contend with in his work of preaching the kingdom. Part of this is a frequent wrestling with unclean spirits and satanic powers that have taken possession of parts of Jewish life and various people. The short passage above is notable in that Bartimaeus, the blind beggar, first signals a new ability to see when he salutes Jesus as "son of David," a Messianic title that has been only on the lips of demons until then. This passage, together with a very similar one in 8:22–26, are also cunningly juxtaposed by Mark to Jesus' attempts to reveal to his disciples who he is and the suffering he must pass through to verify his divine identity and conquer the powers of darkness. As the blind regain their sight, the disciples remain stubbornly rooted in their lack of insight. One of the small details that Mark accentuates is Bartimaeus casting off his cloak (probably his begging shawl). It is a symbol of the leaving behind of the old order. Having done this, Bartimaeus regains his sight and is ready to follow Jesus "on the way," that is, to death and glory in Jerusalem—something the disciples as yet are quite incapable of doing.

Additional Passages

Ez 36:24–31   I will pour cleansing water over you.

Lk 16:19–31   The parable of the rich man and Lazarus.

Questions for Reflection

1. Can I acknowledge times in my life when I was quite blind to the reality of evil with which I was involved?

2. Are there occasions when I realized the presence and action of powers of light or darkness much greater than myself?

3. Do I ever, like Bartimaeus, pray from my depths to be cured of my inability to see?

A Final Thought

Jesus, my friend, you healed a blind man at Bethsaida. He came to you only with the help of his friends. His cure was slow and hesitant. Bartimaeus, in contrast, called out to you and would not be silenced. With new sight came the gift of seeing what was important. Throwing aside all else, he followed you to the end of your battle against the powers of darkness and evil. Help me, Lord, to acknowledge my blindness; make me shout out for your healing touch. Help me to stand on the road and walk with you to Jerusalem, where in my suffering I too will be transfigured in glory.

Day 6
Acknowledging Sin in My Personal History

Prayer Desire

I beg God to know that I am deeply loved even in the worst of my sinful addictions.

Ignatian Focus

As I meditate on my life, I ask for intense and increasing sorrow and tears for my sins. (*The Spiritual Exercises* 55)

Introduction

Perhaps the most extreme image for sin is that of drug addiction. While few of us may have experienced this firsthand, we are familiar with media images of addicts shooting themselves up with heroin or morphine, searching once again for that escape of being high where the burdens of life disappear into oblivion. Such habits often begin in simple ways: sampling a new and forbidden pleasure, discovery of a new world, or release from drudgery and joylessness in dead-end or abusive relationships. What began as adventure or exquisite pleasure can end in self-destruction. Reaching out for comfort and love ends in self-rejection and hatred; this is the heart of addiction.

Most of us have small addictions that we normally keep in check. Yet that perverse longing for love that ends in hatred can run as a subtle motif bringing discord into otherwise harmonious lives. We see this in the dissociation that can afflict many good people, especially when they are discouraged. We remember failures in our lives with vivid recall; we are painfully aware of our responsibility and central place in these fiascoes. If we remember good things, then we stand at a distance and view them dispassionately; we find it difficult to own the love and the wholeness that we were bringing to birth. It may have been God's gift, but we truly created it too. Sin is a parasite—it not only kills; it sucks the sap out of the goodness of life to create a parody of life, a living death.

Ecological Reflection

Some of the fault lines that allow the earth's core to pass its heat out to the surface lie deep down in ocean trenches. Remote-controlled subs with cameras have sent back pictures from such mile-deep canyons. These vents are so deep that no light penetrates; the ocean floor is just mud and rock, bare and lifeless. Yet where these vents pour out their gases and fumes, the beams of light have picked out the most extraordinary living creatures, dancing in the warm currents created there. The pressures are extreme at these depths, and the gases are noxious, deadly to life on land.

These amazing creatures demonstrate that life on our planet has an ability to adapt to the most hostile environments. The inner drives for life and for survival are so resilient. As humans, the physical extremes under which we can survive are narrow. The balance of electrolytes in our blood and gases in our respiratory tracts is very fine-tuned. Yet there is an inner toughness that sees some men and women undergoing long brutal imprisonment and starvation and yet surviving. Long-term addicts give up their heroin or alcohol and become counselors or authors, giving hope to others by retracing the road by which they were able to walk out of these wastelands. In the midst of addiction, life flourishes once again. No matter how deeply engrained our vices have been, Christ's love can bring us new life and hope, something we see St. Paul rejoicing in with his followers at Corinth.

Scripture Reflection: 2 Cor 5:16–21

From now on, therefore, we regard no one from a human point of view; even though we once knew Christ from a human point of view, we know him no longer in that way. So if anyone is in Christ, there is a new creation: everything old has passed away; see, everything has become new! All this is from God, who reconciled us to himself through Christ, and has given us the ministry of reconciliation; that is, in Christ God was reconciling the world to himself, not counting their trespasses against them, and entrusting the message of reconciliation to us. So we are ambassadors for Christ, since God is making his appeal through us; we entreat you on behalf of Christ, be reconciled to God. For our sake he made him to be sin who knew no sin, so that in him we might become the righteousness of God.

Scripture Commentary

Paul's letters to the people of Corinth reveal a pattern common to many passionate relationships: love, betrayal, jealousy, recrimination, and reconciliation. Corinth was a cosmopolitan and feisty seaport, full of vices and excesses. If they had possessed cocaine and heroin, you can be sure that some of Paul's church would have been on them. Though this second letter is disjointed and may carry the scars of several bust-ups and reconciliations, its central message is very clear: Christ's love can grow and flourish even in the worst adversity and opposition.

What was causing so much anguish in Paul is that later preachers seem to have been swaying the church to doctrines that Paul was sure would ultimately lead to self-destruction. These may have been a mixture of wanting to get back to the strict Jewish law or the other extreme of getting high on the Spirit, glorying in ecstatic experiences and miraculous incidents. Paul insists on his authority so as to save the unity of the small and weak community. In this passage he accentuates the unique role that Christ has given to each of his followers. It is to be a missionary of reconciliation. Having been created anew by God's forgiveness in Christ, they must extend that forgiveness to others. To make this message of forgiveness open to everybody, Jesus had become human, one like us in every way except sin. To accept that message of forgiveness and love would be to do away with the rivalries and jealousies that rent the church at Corinth and make new life emerge where dissension seemed to rule.

Additional Passages

Lk 18:9–14   The parable of the Pharisee and the tax collector.
Phil 3:7–15   I regard all things as loss compared to Christ.

Questions for Reflection

1. Which memories tempt you back into despondency? And which bring you life and hope?
2. Is there any addiction that still dogs you? What seems to make it impossible to get rid of it?
3. What survivors of hardship, jealousy, or brutality do you know of whose affirmation of life can still bring hope to those struggling with death or despair?

A Final Thought

In Louisville, at the corner of Fourth and Walnut, in the center of the shopping district, I was suddenly overwhelmed with the realization that I loved all these people, that they were mine and I theirs, that we could not be alien to one another even though we were total strangers. It was like waking from a dream of separateness, of spurious self-isolation in a special world, the world of renunciation and supposed holiness. . . .

It is a glorious destiny to be a member of the human race, though it is a race dedicated to many absurdities and one which makes many terrible mistakes; yet, with all that, God himself glorified in becoming a member of the human race! To think that such a commonplace realization should suddenly seem like news that one holds the winning ticket in a cosmic sweepstake.

—Thomas Merton

Day 7
Sin as Death

Prayer Desire

I beg God to show me how my sins so undermine his beloved world that I have been a carrier of death in it.

Ignatian Focus

I pause in wonder as I see how many other creatures have helped preserve my life, while I have been so narrow and self-serving in my sinfulness. (*The Spiritual Exercises* 60)

Introduction

In his work *Dark Nature,* the biologist Lyall Watson succinctly states that the two rules most deeply written into all animal genetic codes are, first, be nasty to outsiders and, second, be nice to insiders. With a few exceptions, animals do not kill their own species; when they hunt other species, it is to provide food for themselves and their cubs, not for the sheer joy of the hunt. We humans are the only animals on earth that treat one another as if we shared no common origin or bonds. Whether it be the ethnic cleansing that marked the Balkans in the 1980s and 1990s or the Mundurucu headhunters of the Amazon Basin, who categorize all outsiders in the same food group as peccary and tapir, violence is a very widespread human characteristic. Ironically, this tendency flows partly from the weakness and vulnerability of the lone person. In one-to-one confrontation, a single hominoid was never a match for a saber-toothed tiger or a woolly mastodon. Once gathered in clan groups, however, humans over tens of thousands of years learned how to isolate, trap, and then kill such large animals by dint of the weapons they had slowly constructed. In this way they learned to dominate the natural world about them.

The story of human origins in the early chapters of the Book of Genesis offers a subtle theological reflection on this history. Created together, man and woman needed each other to be human; they also needed other animals and plants for their very survival. In their thrust for independence and to rise above their puny physical limitations, they plotted against one another and the world God had given them. Adam and Eve blamed each other for their failures, while Cain killed his brother out of jealousy over his success. This is just the beginning of a long saga of blaming and scapegoating anybody who was too different from the in-group, those in power. In this way sin and death became inextricably intertwined.

Ecological Reflection

In creating a common culture that separates them from all other creatures, humans have evolved three distinctive characteristics: an ability to live a lifestyle virtually independent of their local environment, an extraordinary focus on their inner needs and desires, and the creation of a global economic system. This helps us to understand why so many modern humans seem to have lost any innate sense of limits. When their lives flourish, they seem to ask no questions as to what price is paid for this lifestyle by other creatures or by the ecosystems that lie outside their immediate awareness. If we follow the path of human expansion, we find a trail littered with the destruction of species and environments. The settlement of Australia by aboriginal peoples was followed by the disappearance of the larger species of mammals and lizards. When a land bridge allowed hunters to cross the Bering Straits into the Americas twelve thousand years ago, the remaining Ice Age species, the woolly mammoth, mastodon, giant bison, and woolly rhinoceros, soon vanished. We see the same pattern in Madagascar and Crete. What is unique about the great Minoan culture of Crete was that the hewing down of the forests that provided the planks to adorn their vast palaces led to the erosion of the soil on which the rocky promontories depended for life. Once the tree cover was removed, the soil eroded and the civilization sank into the sea. Volcanic eruption and a tsunami completed the devastation.

The destruction of competing cultures that accompanied such human expansion is not something that has vanished with the growth of modern technology. The nineteenth and twentieth centuries are rife with instances of genocide, from the systematic hunting down of the Tasmanian aboriginals in the 1820s and 1830s to the slaughter of a million Armenian Christians in the second decade of the century past, a crime still downplayed or ignored by official Turkish histories. Such deeply ingrained behaviors have led many anthropologists and sociobiologists to paint a dismal future for the human species. As population and resource pressure on the earth becomes greater and global warming increases, rich and privileged nations will fight to preserve their lifestyle. Plagues, famine, and wars will follow until either the global ecosystem tips out of the balance in which humans can survive or we kill ourselves with nuclear, biological, or chemical weapons. The death of the last human will then fulfill the gloomy words written by James Jeans over seventy years ago (see "A Final Thought," below). In the following passage from Ephesians, Paul reflects how humans were powerless to free themselves from such death-dealing cultures until Christ brought his love into this world.

Scripture Reflection: Eph 2:1–10

You were dead through the trespasses and sins in which you once lived, following the course of this world, following the ruler of the power of the air, the spirit that is at work among those who are disobedient. All of us once lived among them in the passions of our flesh, following the desires of flesh and senses, and we were by nature children of wrath, like everyone else. But God, who is rich in mercy, out of the great love with which he loved us even when we were dead through our trespasses, made us alive together with Christ—by grace you have been saved—and raised us up with him and seated us with him in the heavenly places in Christ Jesus, so that in the ages to come he might show the immeasurable riches of his grace in kindness toward us in Christ Jesus. For by grace you have been saved through faith, and this is not your own doing; it is the gift of God—not the result of works, so that no one may boast. For we are what he has made us, created in Christ Jesus for good works, which God prepared beforehand to be our way of life.

Scripture Commentary

The letter to the Ephesians contains a sweeping vision of God's plan for the human species. It starts from something never envisaged before; that the death of Jesus Christ would bring both Jews and Gentiles into a new unified human race. Because Christ has been given power over the malevolent forces that afflict our planet's history, he is able to free men and women from the immoral and deceitful influences that have filled our world with hatred and division. The new life of believers, one rooted in knowledge and spiritual power, will be in stark contrast to the old life of ignorance and violence. Eventually, Christ will bring about a total reestablishment of God's sovereignty over all creation. Freedom to enter this new life is purely the result of God's grace and utterly precludes any human boasting. Paul is adamant that Christ will eventually remold the pattern of this world because in his rising and exaltation he has already begun to reshape and transfigure the lives of those who believe in him.

Additional Passages

Ez 34:1–16   God's verdict on the false shepherds of Israel.
Mt 25:31–46   The final judgment.

Questions for Reflection

1. Have I ever acted as an agent of death in this world? Do I still?
2. What life have I given to others? Have I created new vision, hope, and growth at different levels of life, biological, cultural, or spiritual?
3. How am I called to continue Christ's work of reconciliation in the place in which I am planted?

A Final Thought

Is this, then, all that life amounts to—to stumble, almost by mistake, into a universe which was clearly not designed for life, and which, to all appearances, is either totally indifferent or definitely hostile to it, to stay clinging onto a fragment of a grain of sand until we are frozen off, to strut on our tiny stage with the knowledge that our aspirations are all but doomed to final frustration, and that our achievements must perish with our race, leaving the universe as though we had never been?

—James Jeans

Day 8
Healing of Sin as Regaining of Sight

Prayer Desire

I humbly ask God to let me see the core of energy and power hidden in the depths of my being.

Ignatian Focus

I gaze upon Christ on the cross dying for love of me, and I ask myself, what have I done for Christ? What am I doing for Christ? What ought I be doing for Christ? (*The Spiritual Exercises* 53)

Introduction

After leaving the shores of New Zealand, Captain Cook's *Endeavour* sailed on to Australia. As the ship drew near the shore of what is now known as Cape Everard in April 1770, the crew saw some aboriginals fishing from their canoes. There was absolutely no reaction until they lowered a whaleboat and starting rowing toward the shore. Only then did the fishermen rush to defend their territory. The aboriginals must have seen something and felt the waves of the ship's passage, but because there was no parallel for them in their experience, they ignored it. In a very real sense they could not see it. As soon, however, as they saw what looked to them like a raiding party, they reacted as they would have to any other threat.

This story gives us a faint inkling of what Ignatius refers to as the mystery of sin. That it is literally something we cannot see until God reveals it to us. Sin is mysterious in that it is a negation of what might have and should have been. What is common to the analogies of blindness, addiction, death is that they all bespeak failures and endings. In each some person or possession has been reduced to a threat or benefit, just an object, something to be manipulated and used, instead of being accepted in the full glory of its being. Sin is literally a hole, a surd, a misrepresentation, the full extent of which we cannot see until God reveals it to us. In contrast, coming closer to God may demand letting go of our partial vision and certainties. Like Cook's aboriginals, we may have to allow something risky and threatening to enter our world if we are to discover the richness of as yet undreamed of worlds.

Ecological Reflection

Most educated adults know that earth is just a tiny spot in an immense universe. Because of superb telescopes such as the Hubble, radio telescopes all networked together, space probes, and the astrophysics built on Einstein's equations, we nonetheless retain a comfortable notion that we have a good grasp of the basic shape and nature of our universe. One feels, nonetheless a hint of uneasiness among professional astronomers when the subject turns to so-called dark matter. Since the 1930s it has become increasingly clearer that we cannot account for all the matter in the universe. The galaxies we observe are all rotating at about twice the speed we would expect given their mass, which we have been fairly sure of calculating. According to Einstein's mathematics, they should be flying apart. New detection methods have revealed huge amounts of superheated gas within galaxies that is invisible to our eyes. Yet this still accounts for only about a third of the mass we need to find to understand why our universe does not fly apart.

A number of solutions were proposed, including dwarf stars and the famous black holes that remain when a large or very large star dies. Yet all these could be detected in various ways. What astronomers now believe is that up to 70 percent of our universe is made up of what is being termed "dark energy," mysterious forces of which we know little. It is clear that there is a very large part of our universe that is inaccessible to human eyes and some, perhaps a large amount, that is utterly beyond any existing instrument to detect or measure.

If our physical world is so mysterious, how much more so the inner realms of God. Sin too is mysterious, for it is an attempt to negate the God who is the ground and meaning of all being, visible and invisible. We see such incomprehension perfectly exemplified in the following story from Luke's gospel.

Scripture Reflection: Lk 12:16–21

Then he told them a parable; "The land of a rich man produced abundantly. And he thought to himself, 'What shall I do, for I have no place to store my crops?' Then he said, 'I will do this: I will pull down my barns and build larger ones, and there I will store all my grain and my goods. And I will say to my soul, "Soul, you have ample goods laid up for many years; relax, eat, drink, be merry." But God said to him, 'You fool! This very night your life is being demanded of you. And the things you have prepared, whose will they be?' So it is with those who store up treasures for themselves but are not rich toward God."

Scripture Commentary

A leading theme in Luke's gospel is his portrayal of Jesus as an embodiment of the compassion of God. We see this in the way he reaches out to those on the margins of Jewish society—tax collectors, the poor, sick, lepers, and prostitutes—more so than in the other gospels. On the other hand, those who would generally have been regarded as favored by God—such as the rich landowner, Dives, or the Pharisee who gave a banquet for Jesus without washing his feet—all of these are depicted as self-deceiving and hypocritical. Luke's different vision of these figures comes from his notion of what it is to be a disciple called by Christ. To be part of God's new kingdom of justice and peace is not something one achieves alone; it is intricately linked with being part of a community of brothers and sisters who live in a way consistent with God's vision of the unity of all humanity. When we listen to this rich farmer, we hear his constant use of "I," and "my," as he sketches a future in which he alone figures. In Luke's Greek it is not so much God that demands his life, but more the goods and possessions that come to claim him. Not only does sin narrow our vision, it reduces us to the things that we covet.

Additional Passages
Jn 12:31–36   Jesus is the light of the world.
Lk 15:11–32   Story of the loving father and his two sons.

Questions for Reflection
1. What are the origins of my image of God? Has it become fixed at any stage?
2. Do I have a barn in which I store my goods and talents as security for my future? Where is this barn stashed?
3. Do I ever check with colleagues or friends to see if they have noticed dark matter in my universe of dreams and fears that does not feature on my internal radar screen?

A Final Thought
Then two wonders happened at the same moment. One was that the voice was suddenly joined by other voices; more voices than you could possibly count. They were in harmony with it, but far higher up the scale: cold, tingling, silvery voices. The second wonder was that the blackness overhead, all at once, was blazing with stars. They didn't come out gently one by one, as they do on a summer evening. One moment there had been nothing but darkness; next moment a thousand, thousand points of light leaped out—single stars, constellations and planets, brighter and bigger than any in our world. There were no clouds. The new stars and the new voices began at exactly the same time. If you had seen and heard it, as Digory did, you would have felt quite certain that it was the stars themselves which were singing and that it was the First Voice, the deep one, which had made them appear and made them sing. . . .

—C. S. Lewis

Day 9
Healing as Freedom Unto Death

Prayer Desire

I pray for the freedom to surrender to death, so as to be able to live now as a free person.

Ignatian Focus

I ask Mary to help me have insight into this world so as to be able to see its vanity and pretense so that I may die to what is false and deceitful in it. (*The Spiritual Exercises* 63)

Introduction

The last twenty-five years have seen a number of books on the topic of near-death experiences. After the initial work by Dr. Raymond Moody, many researchers tracked down people who had shown signs of clinical death but then revived. Stories of seeing bright lights, passing through a tunnel to another realm, and meeting a being of utter love and acceptance proved more common than expected. Specialists in the physiology of the brain began to put forward explanations based on the patterning of electrical circuitry; discussion still wages on. One thing does seem clear. People who have passed through this journey have quite a different stance toward their eventual death. Fear has passed; instead there is a sense that what awaits them is not dread or annihilation, but rather some deep fulfillment.

This intuition links into Ignatius's views on death and sin. His treatment of sin is not relational or psychological as in the pattern of most modern writing. It is totally theocentric, or God-centered. In that perspective, sin is an act of enormous ingratitude and irreverence for God. It totally subverts the order and purpose of creation and so will inevitably lead to the death of the sinner, but for the intervention of God's mercy. That is why Ignatius's treatment of the fall of the angels, the sin of Adam and Eve, and the thrusting down to hell of a sinner for one mortal sin seems so harsh to modern readers. In today's parlance, what Ignatius seems to propose is that sin is like someone saying, "I will never die, and I would refuse to walk down a tunnel to such a meeting," no matter what.

Fear of death may rest on someone being secretly in thrall to another god that they have made the be all and end all of their life. Or it may be that they have known instances of loss or rejection so deep they have never been resolved; therefore they are not ready to meet death. In his work *The Denial of Death* Ernest Becker suggested that many people conceal such fears by taking on "projects of immortality," crusades so all-important that they will outlive even their personal demise. These may be a consuming passion for a work project, a personal dream, or some cult hero whose image will outlast death. It may be some burden from the past that will survive even death; one's children may have to inherit the quest. One of the great fruits of meeting the unconditional mercy of God in the first week of the Exercises is that we are able to let go. We can be freed from such life-consuming drives, for Christ in dying has released us from the burden and fear of death.

Ecological Reflection

A charge against ecological concern is that it is a luxury for guilt-ridden First-World citizens. Only wealthy middle-class people with lots of time and extra energy are able to go out on crusades to save the spotted owl or lesser-crested snail darter. Poor people who have to struggle against harsh environments simply to live do not have such a romantic view of nature. Whatever truth there may be in such accusations, it is also a fact that botanists and zoologists who work in the field have no illusions about the harsh face of nature. Such are Annie Dillard's observations about the lethal bite of the giant water bugs that she watched at Tinker Creek or Lyall Watson's description of newborn hyenas. Normally born as twins, they are already completely furred, with eyes open and razorlike teeth ready for action. Within minutes of birth one twin will attack the other in a battle to the death; sometimes this happens while they are still in the amniotic sac. Such students of nature know that they are seeing such a thrust and passion for life in a world wherein competition for food and mates can be urgent. Death is life's ever present handmaiden. In his letter to the people of Corinth, Paul also accepts how close life and death walk in the everyday struggles of Christian living.

Scripture Reflection: 2 Cor 4:7–18

But we have this treasure in clay jars, so that it may be made clear that this extraordinary power belongs to God and does not come from us. We are afflicted in every way, but not crushed; perplexed, but not driven to despair; persecuted, but not forsaken; struck down, but not destroyed; always carrying in the body the death of Jesus, so that the life of Jesus may also be visible in our bodies. For while we live, we are always being given up to death for Jesus' sake, so that the life of Jesus may be made visible in our mortal flesh. So death is at work in us, but life in you.

But just as we have the same spirit of faith that is in accordance with scripture—"I believed and so I spoke"—we also believed, and so we speak, because we know that the one who raised the Lord Jesus will raise us also with Jesus, and will bring us with you into his presence. Yes, everything is for your sake, so that grace, as it extends to more and more people, may increase thanksgiving, to the glory of God.

So we do not lose heart. Even though our outer nature is wasting away, our inner nature is being renewed day by day. For this slight momentary affliction is preparing us for the eternal weight of glory beyond all measure, because we look not at what can be seen but at what cannot be seen; for what can be seen is temporary, but what cannot be seen is eternal.

Scripture Commentary

All of us experience how weak we are on occasion. Despite this, the overcoming of such adversity shows the extent of God's power working in us. The death of Jesus is mirrored in our bodily sufferings, but this highlights even more the inner life of Christ that keeps on growing within us. The part of us that undergoes such afflictions and sufferings is like an exoskeleton, an outer skin. While it wears away, our inner being is constantly strengthened and renewed. Whenever in our day-to-day life we come across death, we are reminded of the resurrection of Christ, so robbing death of its power to master us.

Additional Passages

Is 54:4–10   Yahweh as a husband.

Lk 7:36–50   The woman who washes Jesus' feet.

Questions for Reflection

1. What has been my experience of death? Has it left me afraid?
2. Can I identify any project of immortality in my own life? Or one carried by my wider family?
3. Do I have models of loved ones passing courageously to their Maker that can give me hope?

A Final Thought

If something hurts me, the hurts I suffered back then come back to me, and when I feel guilty, the feelings of guilt return; if I yearn for something today, or feel homesick, I feel the yearnings and homesickness from back then. The tectonic layers of our lives rest so tightly one on top of another that we always come up against earlier events in later ones, not as matter that has been fully formed and pushed aside, but absolutely present and alive.

—Bernard Schlink

Her hair poured in coils of jet,
hiding the head once so neat,
undulating to the tide of tears
as she kissed and dried his feet.
The Pharisees hissed harlot in her ear,
and I did too, for I also had been there.
But then I knew I was kneeling,
weeping for my sins and lies,
for the covetous selling of my talents
and the drops of praise I could prize.
Seducing hearts was her art and mine,
she for lust, I under cover of love divine.
Oh how I too longed to be pampered
and among the discerning to be prized,

to have that apparent triumph
to manipulate and yet to despise.
But the worst of our lies was within
to keep seeing needs and never sin.
My ointment I poured with abandon
not caring where it might flow,
grasping my chance for freedom,
to cling and never let go.
—A commentary on Lk 7:36–50

Day 10
Trusting in the Freedom of His Love

Prayer Desire

I ask God to open my eyes to my dignity and freedom as a child of God, as both a creature and cocreator of the universe.

Ignatian Focus

I beg that all my actions and their intentions may flow purely out of desire for the praise and majesty of God. (*The Spiritual Exercises* 46)

Introduction

Commentators on the Exercises agree that the focus of the first week is not on sin but on the absolute gratuitousness of God's forgiveness of sin. It is not an effort to analyze the nature or causes of the retreatant's sins. Rather, the stress is on begging God to reveal the effects of sin, even to bring one to tears for them—but again this is not an exercise in guilt or shame. It is an attempt to free the one making the Exercises from pointless attempts to probe the meaning of sin or bolster the will against it. It is more an unshackling of the imagination so as to enter into God's love for a distorted world, to be taken up into his redemptive heart, aching because of the degradation and self-inflicted torment of so many of his children. Part of that process is for the retreatant to see how much his or her personal history is of a piece with the rest of humankind.

Beginning to taste God's personal call to mercy, the retreatant will also begin to see the beauty and graciousness of God in all the world around. Being moved to see with God's eyes also allows an objectivity to accept that I was not, or never will be, the center of the world or universe. God's love extends to all history and all creatures. My part in that is unique—but limited. A sense of shame often accompanies this regaining of moral vision. This is not wallowing in guilt or burdening ourselves with our ancestors' mistakes or lack of vision. Rather it can be embraced with gratitude, for it fills us with the hope that we will not repeat the same mistakes. Finally, the gift of the Spirit, blowing through the retreatants' understanding, will give each of them the special gift of seeing the particularity, distinctiveness, and uniqueness of each of God's creatures within the vast unity that is creation. This brings liberation—freedom from egotism and slavery to objects or achievements to bolster a weak sense of identity or belonging.

Ecological Reflection

Near the end of the eighteenth century the French mathematician Pierre Laplace made an extraordinary claim about the future. If science were given enough information to know precisely the laws of nature and a map of where all objects were situated, "nothing would be uncertain, and the future as the past would be present to its eyes." This statement probably marks the high tide of determinism, that is, the claim that everything that occurs is shaped by precise, unwavering physical laws; understand those laws and all events become predictable and controllable. Though few scientists today would put forward such a claim, still in Western culture there is an undefined but pervasive notion that scientific advances will eventually allow us humans to know most of what is significant and important in our world and universe.

More sober minds acknowledge that there is still a vast amount we do not know about our universe and its ultimate fate. The nature of dark matter, the age and size of the universe, whether it will fly apart, expand infinitely, or eventually collapse in on itself in a huge crunch:

not only do we not know the answers to these questions; we may never know them. Part of the reason for this is the realization that what happens in our world arises from a combination of fixed laws and unpredictable random events. The last fifty years have brought a far deeper knowledge of fractals, patterns in nature like those found in clouds, coastlines, and snowflakes, all following a common pattern but subtly different, a mixture of order and disorder. Then there is the famous chaos theory, which shows us how many processes in the natural world follow predictable patterns and cycles until tiny incremental changes eventually trigger an enormous fluctuation leading to a heart attack, a plague of locusts, or a new Ice Age. The role of individual players and events can therefore redirect the whole course of history. An oft-repeated example is how General Robert E. Lee's one bad military decision during the battle of Gettysburg changed the entire course of the Civil War. From a string of successes where the South could nearly sue for an honorable peace, it was staring at failure and defeat.

We humans are not just the passive playthings of global history; while being shaped by it we are also making it happen. This is part of what it is to be in the image of God, indeed a co-creator of the world and cosmic history. In this passage from Ephesians, Paul rejoices at the high dignity to which we are all called because of our being made part of the risen and cosmic Christ.

Scripture Reflection: Eph 1:15–23

I have heard of your faith in the Lord Jesus and your love toward all the saints, and for this reason I do not cease to give thanks for you as I remember you in my prayers. I pray that the God of Our Lord Jesus Christ, the Father of glory, may give you a spirit of wisdom and revelation as you come to know him, so that, with the eyes of your heart enlightened, you may know what is the hope to which he has called you, what are the riches of his glorious inheritance among the saints, and what is the immeasurable greatness of his power for us who believe, according to the working of his great power. God put this power to work in Christ when he raised him from the dead and seated him at his right hand in the heavenly places, far above all rule and authority and power and dominion, and above every name that is named, not only in this age but also in the age to come. And he has put all things under his feet and has made him the head over all things for the church, which is his body, the fullness of him who fills all in all.

Scripture Commentary

In this passage Paul gives thanks for and with the church at Ephesus. Now the Christians there are able to comprehend their true dignity in Christ. For having conquered the dark powers of this world, Jesus has been taken from this earth to a place of exaltation. Because Christians also share in his death and rising, the Ephesians can be confident that they too will have a place in the renewed creation. Already they join with the angels in a heavenly liturgy together with the risen Jesus, head of the body which is his church.

Additional Passages

Lk 15:1–7   The parable of the lost sheep.
Jn 10:1–15   Jesus is the good shepherd caring for his flock.

Questions for Reflection

1. In what ways have you begun to know God's mercy and forgiveness in a new way during this first week of the Exercises?
2. Do you begin to see the world of creation about you in a new light?
3. Does some new call from God begin to awaken in you, or the reaffirmation of a mission that has already been entrusted to you?

A Final Thought

It was getting near home time and a storm had begun. One little lass had a long way to go down dark lanes. I worried for her and asked if I should go with her. She refused my help with a smile, 'There was no need, she would be all right, she was not afraid.' It was only at the last moment that I could relax, for her father arrived to take her home. She came over to me. 'I know Daddy was coming for me and he has brought me a new coat.' I watched them as they walked out the door together; she looked so radiant.

Much later I realized what a marvelous picture this was of the Christian facing death. We cannot avoid the storm or the dark, but we are not alone and we shall be given a 'new coat'. We may not know what lies ahead, but we know Who.

—An Irish tale

Week 2 *Two*

BIRTH AND EPIPHANY

The first week of *The Spiritual Exercises* is about finding freedom through rediscovering God's love for us. God has called us out of sin into a new sense of freedom. Ignatius's second week is about the discovery of our true identity and mission in life. This is far more than what sort of job I am best skilled for or even finding a community and project to which I can make a significant contribution that brings me personal satisfaction. During this week the Exercises will bring me to a place where I hear God call me by a particular name, one that is new to me. This will not only help me see my entire life in a new perspective; it will also provide me with a deep sense of where God is calling me.

This will not be laid out like a blueprint, an architect's draft for the building of a new house. What God will offer me will be more like a superbly written mystery novel. Each page will provide a new twist, some seeming to lead nowhere, others painful and frustrating. At times the characters make poor decisions and wrong alliances, but as I race toward the conclusion, it dawns on me that the first pages held the subtle clues pointing to the denouement. I begin to see with utter clarity how God has been with me, helping to shape my life into something more than I could ever have hoped and dreamed it could be.

This blueprint is the life story of Jesus Christ. It is as if he is at my side as my personal tutor, or as if I am an apprentice and he is the master artisan. I am constantly learning from studying the pattern of his life, a pattern found in the pages of the New Testament. Yet it is not as if he were some distant authoritative teacher. Rather, it is a constantly repeated discovery that the pattern that he provides has already been shaping my goals and decisions all along, from within.

Some readers, who have begun to widen their vision to take on the ecological perspective of God and the universe drawn in the first chapter, may wonder if this pattern involves returning to the Hebrew world-view of twenty centuries ago, which saw the earth as a flattened dish surrounded by the hemisphere of the heavens. Since we know the story of Jesus Christ so well and he is now the risen Lord and cosmic Christ, should not our focus be on his drawing forth of a new heaven and a new earth?

To answer this question, we need to remind ourselves that the gospels and letters of the New Testament were not written as historical chronicles studying a dead Jesus. They were primarily witnesses of faith, preparing Christians for the second coming of Jesus, his rule at the end of time. They aimed to help Christians to understand and prepare for a dangerous future by offering a key to the past in the life and death of Jesus. There is a saying, "God has no contemporaries." It points to the truth that God had no need of anything or anybody outside the persons of the Trinity to abide in the fullness of being and bliss. In deciding to create this universe, God changed that equation. In becoming a human, one of us, Jesus Christ changed the history of God.

When Mary became pregnant with Jesus, God entered time—our time. That meant that he had to wait on people, in both senses of that word. God's eternal plans now became subject to the constraints of human time: birth, growing up, delayed decisions, premature deaths. In becoming a fetus, Jesus submitted God to the biological time clock. Through his DNA, Jesus took on not just Mary's biological past but the genetic inheritance of the Semitic peoples. He also took on the human evolutionary past. He inherited chemical bonds laid down in the cooling of supernovae, structures that developed in plants, muscle and tissue structure found in animals, and finally the embodied spirit unique to human creatures. In taking on this inheritance, he became connected to every being at every level of this entire cosmos. Though the gospels could not have articulated this mystery in the scientific framework that we now employ, they are full of awareness that the fate of Jesus is tied to the purpose and outcomes of this universe.

In studying the earthly life of Jesus, we gain access to a privileged and definitive insight into the inner life of God and what God's intentions are for this world and this universe. Obviously, we see this in Jesus' teaching and his acts of power. Yet in a very particular way it is his entire life history that gives us the best clues about how to live as a free and loving child of God. Many retreatants are surprised to discover how many hours Ignatius sets aside for contemplating the mysteries of Jesus' early childhood and growing up. It seems particularly odd because the literary forms used in these sections of the gospels of Matthew and Luke are quite different from the literary forms used in the rest of their writing. They are much more symbolic and shaped by cultural myths and story forms. As we will see, both Luke and Matthew use the stories of Jesus' early years as minigospels and minicreation accounts, creating links with early Jewish origins and giving hints as to the future shape of Jesus' life.

In a strange way these literary forms give superb scope to Ignatian prayer forms, especially in the use of active imagination. Because the authors were not so interested in the historical details of stories like the visit of the magi or Jesus' flight into Egypt as they were in the symbolical and biblical significance of these events, this leaves a huge scope to the creative power of the readers' imaginations. We know too that in early childhood the growth of the power of imagination is critical in the awakening of wonder, curiosity, and hope in developing minds and bodies. In allowing their inner senses of imagination, memory, and creativity to make these childhood stories of Jesus flower within them, retreatants are also shaping themselves and developing the skills that will allow them to enter with empathy and openness into the later stories of Jesus' teaching and miracles.

In opening all their inner senses to the stories of Jesus' childhood and early ministry, those making the Exercises come to see profound links and similarities between their own family of origin and its interrelationships and the same issues in the life of Christ. In making such linkages, they also realize that they are being invited to share his rich life of communion with the other members of the Trinity, with his Father and the Holy Spirit. Learning to hear the Father's call as Jesus did is the way to discover what are the truly good inspirations of our life and what are illusions. This contemplation of Christ's youth also trains us to discern what is the special mission and destiny that God has for each of us personally in this world. This is the work of the second week of our retreat.

Day 11
The God of Surprises

Prayer Desire
I ask for trust in God so as to be totally open to his gifts.

Ignatian Focus
Our first task is to see the persons of Jesus' childhood with the eye of the imagination, meditating upon and grasping their situation, surroundings, and inner world, and gathering fruit from these insights. (*The Spiritual Exercises* 122)

Introduction
History books often dwell on the lives of the great persons from the past. Historians like Tacitus or philosophers like Seneca or Cicero are caught up in the intrigues of court or the debates within the senate. The conspiracies of leaders and the victories of generals are their stock-in-trade and define their world. The Christian gospels breathe a different air. Most often their leading characters are the refugees of history: insignificant old people like Anna or Simeon, the socially shunned such as lepers or shepherds, young village girls like Mary of Nazareth. When God became a human among us, it is with such seemingly insignificant people that he shared the news of his coming. Why? One factor is that, to the powerful, knowledge is power; it is the power to plot, circumvent, and use every scrap of advance warning to position themselves better from risk of betrayal. Such will be the tactics of King Herod the Great in hearing rumors of the birth of Jesus. The poor,

however, are often in no position to make use of what they might over-hear. They lack the contacts and the bargaining power. Instead, like the shepherds in the night fields of Bethlehem, they can just look up at the star and the heavenly host, marvel, and rush off to share the wonder and joy in their hearts with whoever is willing to listen.

Ecological Reflection

The DNA that every human being inherits from his or her mother is only about a tenth of 1 percent different from what comes from their father. And each person differs by about the same amount from every other human on this planet. Biologically speaking, it is very small but very significant. It makes each person utterly unique. Yet more significantly, the huge differences that exist between diverse ethnic and racial groups are much more the result of environment and culture than genetics. Each human being is an exquisite mosaic, made up of innumerable tiny tiles, both biological and cultural, that define this individual's uniqueness. There is no way of knowing in advance which of these inherited gifts is going to be most important for the future well-being and happiness of a person's life and offspring. Here in the South Pacific, study of the mitochondria of Polynesian women has shown that all now living are descendants of just five women from the island of Samoa. At the time, these women could not have had the least suspicion of just how important their lives of hard struggle were to be. The interplay of biology and history is just one of the instruments that the God of surprises uses to draw peoples toward the outworking of his plans for the universe.

Scripture too carries this same witness—that seemingly insignificant events witnessed by simple people in isolated places turn out to be the events on which the whole history and salvation of the world hinge.

Scripture Reflection: Lk 2:8–20

In that region there were shepherds living in the fields, keeping watch over their flock by night. Then an angel of the Lord stood before them, and the glory of the Lord shone around them, and they were terrified. But the angel said to them, "Do not be afraid; for see—I am bringing you good news of great joy for all the people: to you is born this day in the city of David a Savior, who is the Messiah, the Lord. This will be a sign for you: you will find a child wrapped in bands of cloth and lying in a manger." And suddenly there was with the angel a multitude of the heavenly host, praising God and saying, "Glory to God in the highest heaven, and on earth peace among those whom he favors!" When the angels had left them and gone into heaven, the shepherds said to one another, "Let us go now to Bethlehem and see this thing that has taken place, which the Lord has made known to us." So they went with haste and found Mary and Joseph, and the child lying in the manger. When they saw this, they made known what had been told them about this child; and all who heard it were amazed at what the shepherds told them. But Mary treasured all these words and pondered them in her heart. The shepherds returned, glorifying and praising God for all they had heard and seen, as it had been told them.

Scripture Commentary

In his gospel, Luke presents Jesus as the universal Savior of humankind, bringing to fulfillment the promises of salvation, peace, and wholeness of life that are contained in the Old Testament. Luke's gospel, and his second work, the Acts of the Apostles, can be seen as moving outward through a set of concentric circles centered on Jerusalem, Judea, and Rome, all bisected by a common axis, events in each place profoundly touching the others. The story begins in Jerusalem in the Temple, not with the high priests but with Zechariah, a zealous priest from the hill country of Judea. From humble and hidden origins, the story of the rise of Jesus moves from Judea to Galilee and back to Jerusalem; at each stage the fame and influence of Jesus grows. In his inaugural sermon in his home synagogue in Nazareth, Jesus makes clear his agenda of bringing liberation to all those who long for a restoration of true justice in Palestine. More and more he finds that this mission is rejected by the wealthy and privileged but is heard by the poor and marginalized of Jewish society. Jesus' ministry becomes increasingly one of compassion coming from the anointing that he has received from the Holy Spirit.

This passage foreshadows many of these themes. God's messengers come not to Herod's court or the Temple but to shepherds on a bleak hillside. The pastoral and nomadic cast of their work left them open to ritual impurity and neglect of their religious duties, so as a group they were despised. Yet it is to them that the angels announce the epic news. In verse 11 we find the three great titles that Christians were later to bestow on Jesus of Nazareth, Savior, Messiah, and Lord, the last of these being the very word that the Greek translation of the Hebrew scriptures (the Septuagint) used to translate the personal name of God (YHWH), a name so revered that it could not be spoken by devout Jews. The power of Jesus' name and of his proclamation is so great that the good news continues to spread. In Luke's second book, Acts of the Apostles, the Christian gospel, animated by the power of the Spirit, not only leaps over national boundaries but also breaks through previous racial taboos. Beginning in Jerusalem, Acts ends in Rome. The news was first heard by devout Jews, but it had begun to be received even by the diverse and polyglot peoples found in Rome. Just as the first persecution of the church in Jerusalem had led to the gospel being spread throughout Asia and Europe, so the persecution begun under Nero in A.D. 68 (soon after the conclusion of Acts) would send Christianity further out into the Roman world. God's good news shared with the ordinary and insignificant becomes increasingly the hope of renewal and freedom throughout the world.

Additional Passages

Jn 1:1–5; 9–14   The Word becomes flesh and lives among us.
Heb 10:4–10   I have come to do your will, O Lord.

Questions for Reflection

1. How did the knowledge of the good news of Jesus come to my ancestors or to my family?
2. In what ways has my journey of faith been unique and differed from other members of my faith family?
3. What personal gifts of mine act as signs of the good news of the gospel in my life?

A Final Thought

God's activity in the course of saving history is not a kind of monologue which God conducts by himself; it is a long, dramatic dialogue between God and his creatures, in which God confers on man the power to make a genuine answer to his Word, and so makes his own further Word dependent upon the way in which man does in fact freely answer.

—Karl Rahner

Day 12
The God of Fertility

Prayer Desire

I beg God that, just like Mary, I will let the seed of God grow to fullness within me.

Ignatian Focus

While the world is wrapped in violence, Mary is listening to the angel, humbling herself and giving thanks for what God is asking of her. (*The Spiritual Exercises* 108)

Introduction

Friends of mine, Peter and Rosemary, had borne a grief throughout their married life. Despite years of effort, they had not been able to conceive a child. The doctors could find no specific problem, but eventually recommended that they look for some other avenue to have a family. They decided to adopt, and after going through extensive checks and interviews gained a newborn son through open adoption. Their joy was great, but it seemed to make them ache even more for a child of their own bodies. After long deliberation they decided to undergo IVF; they were fortunate, and on their first procedure Rosemary conceived twins. About fifteen months later, I was stunned to get a call from Rosemary saying she was pregnant—despite the doctors' forecasts. Once childless, they now had four children under the age of five. Their joy, and the subsequent rearrangement of their working lives (both were professionals), underlined for me the crucial role of fertility for couples. It also was a reminder that fertility is a key biblical theme.

Just as technologically assisted reproduction and cloning are huge moral issues now, so fertility or the lack of it is a constant theme in the Jewish scriptures. Historical books such as Joshua and Judges show deep concern over the influence on the new Jewish settlers of Syro-Phoenician fertility cults centered around the goddess Astarte. Baal, whom Elijah so derides and mocks in 1 Kings was also a god of fertility. Such cults were still influential in Jesus' time. The riot of the silversmiths recorded in Acts 19 happened because Ephesus was a leading shrine for the goddess Artemis (or Diana), a fertility goddess. Apparently, so many people were being converted to Christianity that it was causing a drop-off in the sale of figurines of the many-breasted goddess. Though fertility was crucial in Jewish life, it could not be won by commerce with the gods, or the temple prostitutes who acted for them, or by magic. It was something bestowed by Yahweh. Prayer might elicit it, but magic never could. Having many children has always been important in clan-based agricultural societies, but for a Jewish woman there was also the pious hope that she might be chosen to be the mother of the Messiah.

The Bible reflects the dominant Jewish view that fertility is a blessing and sterility a curse, yet at times God confounds such stereotyped views. We see the high state and praise won by long-childless women such as Sarah and Hannah, paralleled by the figures of Elizabeth and Mary in the New Testament. They highlight the issue that human conception is not just a biological reality, but a domain of grace too. It is profoundly tied up with God's hopes for humanity. In Christianity, the gift of fertility takes on a new dimension. Every Christian, whether male or female, married or single, parent or childless, must in a certain way be pregnant with Christ and bear him for the life of the world.

Ecological Reflection

One of the most stunning sights to be seen in tropical oceans is the propagation of the coral reefs. At certain optimal conditions, and at a given moment, all the tiny corals spawn. The mass of eggs is so great that the entire area of the sea turns rosy pink and red. It is as if the ocean's cerulean blue has became besmirched and shot through with blood. Frogs too apparently pour out hundreds of eggs with little effort. However, it seems to be that the more complex the creature the more demanding the cost of reproducing itself. This is especially true of humans. I recall being shocked, when doing research for a course on marriage, to discover the proportion of women who died in childbirth in primitive hospitals in early-nineteenth-century Europe. So-called childbed fever, botched breech deliveries, and nursing infections made childbirth a huge risk for many women. Though danger to a mother's life is less today, birth is still an act of faith and love. Consider that up to a third of a mother's life will be committed to the rearing and education of children. Among humans birth is far more than biology; it is a coming close to the divine power of creating.

Scripture Reflection: Lk 1:39–45

In those days Mary set out and went with haste to a Judean town in the hill country, where she entered the house of Zechariah and greeted Elizabeth. When Elizabeth heard Mary's greeting, the child leaped in her womb. And Elizabeth was filled with the Holy Spirit and exclaimed with a loud cry, "Blessed are you among women and blessed is the fruit of your womb. And why has this happened to me, that the mother of my Lord comes to me? For as soon as I heard the sound of your greeting, the child in my womb leaped for joy. And blessed is she who believed that there would be a fulfillment of what was spoken to her by the Lord."

Scripture Commentary

This brief passage is richly allusive. It links Mary to some of the great heroines of the Hebrew scriptures, while the meeting of John and Jesus, even in utero, brings closure to the world of the Jewish prophets to usher in the promised Messianic kingdom. Elizabeth's designation of Mary as the most blessed of all woman is an unmistakable reference to Jael, who pinned the head of the Canaanite general Sisera to the ground with his own tent peg, and Judith, who chopped off the head of the Assyrian general Holofernes. Both achieved what Jewish armies and kings could not. Mary is also greeted as "mother of the Lord." This was the title given to the queen mother as a token of respect and also indicated the special sway she could exercise through her son. That son, Jesus, is already given the title of Lord by Elizabeth, though he is yet to be born. Elizabeth's deference in the face of this illustrious visitor also echoes the fear and respect of King David when the proposal was made to bring into Jerusalem the ark of the covenant, the holy shrine of the presence of the tablets of the law, that had just been won back in battle from the Philistines (2 Sm 6:9).

The creative power of the Spirit that had hovered at the first creation and covered the ark of the covenant also led the two children to acknowledge each other's presence. It likewise prompted Elizabeth to interpret John's leaping within her, the greatest prophet of the Old Testament greeting with joy the one who would inaugurate the New Testament. Mary too is praised in her turn as the model believer who would be blessed because of her trust in the God who had called her.

Additional Passages

Mt 2:1–12	The wise men visit the Christ child.
1 Jn 1:1–4	We give thanks for the word of life.

Questions for Reflection

1. How can I best thank my parents for the gift of life they have handed on to me?
2. How are fertility and the gift of life best articulated in my own life?
3. What are some of the ways I can deepen my relationship with Mary, the mother of my Lord, who has set out to visit me?

A Final Thought

When Mary was carrying my Savior,
I wonder what thoughts filled her head.
Did she wonder how much pain she'd endure,
or was that a question left unsaid.

Did she ask where food and a roof were to come from,
was she anxious that Joseph might not cope,
or how did a country girl raise a prodigy,
or were these things she accepted in hope.
Mary, only you could tell us these answers
and I guess you just said "let it be"
but this Christmas these questions return
for now you are carrying me.
When you were heavy with Jesus,
his was the face you must have yearned to see,
now I long to be born from you
to behold the Neil I was meant to be.

***

A baby is God's opinion that the world should go on.

—Carl Sandburg

Day 13
Growing Up

Prayer Desire

I ask God to show me the unhealed roots of my family's past that I still carry within me so that he may begin to heal them.

Ignatian Focus

As I ponder on the Word becoming one like me, I may want to rest quietly with Jesus and Mary, savoring my relationship with them, begging to know Christ better and follow him more closely. (*The Spiritual Exercises* 104)

Introduction

Early in the second week of the Exercises, Ignatius suggests that each retreatant spends hours reflecting on at least some, if not all, of these gospel passages: the annunciation (Lk 1:26–38), the nativity (Lk 2:1–7), the presentation in the Temple (Lk 2:22–39), the obedience of

Jesus (Lk 2:39–40, 51–52), and his loss and finding in the Temple (Lk 2:41–50). For other retreatants, directors may also suggest the flight into Egypt and massacre of the innocent babies by Herod (Mt 2:13–18) or the visit of the magi to the stable in Bethlehem (Mt 2:1–12).

What Ignatius must have grasped by his long meditation on these passages is that the evangelists used these nativity tales both as mini-gospels capsulizing the whole story of Jesus and as commentary and reflections on the creation stories. First, Jesus is revealed as Savior of the world (not just the Jews) in his self-revelation to the shepherds and the magi. He is rejected by secular powers (Herod), leading to unjust execution (the slaughter of the innocents). The infancy stories are full of hints of the first creation and the calling into being of Israel as a people. The Spirit who overshadows Mary in Lk 1:35 reminds us of the creative power of God in Gn 1:2 and underlines that this child is a totally new creation, the work of God alone. The angels sing blessing over the shepherds in pointed contrast to the fate of the first shepherd, Abel, whose blood soaked the earth. That crime caused the earth to refuse to produce fruit for Cain (Gn 4:10–12), so fulfilling the curse of Gn 3:17–18. In contrast, Jesus is the first fruits of the new creation (1 Cor 15:20–28) who comes into the world to bless work, using the harvest as a symbol of the bounty of God, of the Father's care and mercy.

Ignatius probably did not make all these literary associations consciously. Nevertheless, he implicitly felt the power of the dramatic irony concealed in these childhood vignettes of Jesus' life. For to the open mind these scenes will inevitably suggest questions such as the following: Was my birth humble, poor, and unnoticed? If so, in whose eyes? My parents, mine, or God's? Did other innocent people suffer because I was born? Can I see God's hand in that now? When did I begin to hear God's call in my life? Did I leave home and parents in response to that or for other reasons? Have I ever fully resolved that departure so that I can bring my childhood to God, free from any doubts, fears, and hurts it left in me?

This is where the active imagination is so powerful and creative. Many retreatants have found new self-acceptance being dandled on Mary's knee or playing on the carpentry floor with Jesus and Joseph. This can then lead them to see the hidden graces and pains of their parents' lives, and the grains of sand planted in their own psyches. Some of these may have been transmuted into pearls, other into ulcers. This time may also provide great insight into the struggles of Jesus growing up in an agonistic society, that is, one where roles and behavior are so defined by tradition and the need to preserve family honor that the attempt to create a different life and calling is seen as betrayal and madness (Mk 3:20–21, 6:1–6). Only after Jesus had seemed to reject those near and dear to him (and what did that cost him?) did he have the freedom to call his mother and other women to be his disciples and close friends (Jn 2:1–12, 12:1–8, 19:26–27).

Ecological Reflection

Some cultural anthropologists in New Zealand have made an interesting observation about how mixed groups respond when asked to introduce themselves briefly. Most *pakeha* (nonindigenous New Zealanders), especially men, will tell the group their job, for example, I am an accountant working for Standard and Poors. They may then say, I am married with two children. Many Maori will begin by saying "*I am Ngati Porou* (a tribe from the East Coast of the North Island), *and my mountain is Hikurangi*" (the dominant peak in this area). They may then go on to tell the group their *hapu* (subtribe) and about their extended family in the area in which they grew up. Most Maori still have a keen awareness of their genealogy, back for many generations. They explain who they are by drawing their significant relationships, and this includes the land in which their family grew up (though this is changing somewhat as more and more Maori grow up in cities).

We note that this is just how Matthew introduces Jesus (Mt 1:1–17), through his genealogy, presenting it in three groups of fourteen names to accentuate how Jesus is truly a son of Abraham and a son of David. In contrast, many of us Westerners tend to define ourselves by the work we do or the desirable area we have now moved into. It seems hardly any wonder then that many retreatants even well into their lives can still feel unrooted, unsure of who they are and therefore why they are there. Where they grew up is just part of childhood memories.

Scripture Reflection: Mt 2:16–21

When Herod saw he had been tricked by the wise men, he was infuriated, and he sent and killed all the children in and around Bethlehem who were two years old or under, according to the time that he had learned from the wise men. Then was fulfilled what had been spoken through the prophet Jeremiah: "A voice was heard in Ramah, wailing and loud lamentation, Rachel weeping for her children; she refused to be consoled, because they were no more." When Herod died, an angel of the Lord suddenly appeared in a dream to Joseph and said, "Get up, take the child and his mother, and go the land of Israel, for those who were seeking the child's life are dead." Then Joseph got up, took the child and his mother, and went to the land of Israel.

Scripture Commentary

Matthew sees Jesus' childhood as a pointer to his call as the new Moses, the bringer of God's new covenant. Not so surprisingly, he takes this story about Jesus' childhood and tries to highlight for his readers its Messianic colorings. The slaughter of the innocents evokes the death of the newborn in Egypt at the time of Moses, but more significantly it allows the evangelist to speak of the child Jesus' return from a time of exile in that country. In this way he is like Moses (and the people of Israel), whom the Lord carried out of Egypt like a child (see Hos 11:1). The picture of Rachel weeping for her lost children takes us instantly to the prophet Jeremiah (31:15). The great foremother is weeping for her children of the Northern Kingdom who have been carried into exile in Babylon. But as we read on a few verses, the prophet begins to promise a great restoration, inaugurated by a new covenant written not in tablets of stone but in the heart. Matthew is pointing to Jesus as the one destined to bring about this new covenant.

Additional Passages

Lk 2:41–50   Jesus is lost in Jerusalem.

Phil 2:1–5   Be of one heart and one mind with Christ.

Questions for Reflection

1. Where do I find my sense of identity? Through work? Family? Wider relationships?
2. Am I aware of my genealogy, and the familial blessings and failures that may still be playing out unconsciously through me?
3. What steps should I take after this retreat to make reconciliation with the ghosts of my past?

A Final Thought

The "axle of strength" is found in the Maori use of the *whakapapa* (genealogy). This is a means of affirming identity, linking the speaker with his hearers and with the past, so that it also becomes a statement of the meaning of history. It has become a truism to say that Western man since Descartes draws his identity from within himself, "I think, therefore I am," whereas the Maori speaker says, "I belong, therefore I am." The *whakapapa* tells the story of the speaker by saying where he comes from, and at the same time enables his listeners to identify common ancestors and common tribal affiliations. Identity is found in belonging.

—James Irwin

Day 14
Jesus Is Baptized

Prayer Desire

I ask Jesus that I may enter with him into his experience of baptism so as to know myself ever more deeply as God's beloved.

Ignatian Focus

One of the greatest gifts I can receive is an intimate knowledge of Christ, who made himself human for me; this gift will allow me to better love and follow him. (*The Spiritual Exercises* 104)

Introduction

For some time now the religious order to which I belong has sent our candidates, in their fifth year of training, to spend two years in a foreign culture, for instance, Brazil, the Philippines, or Fiji. Part of the reasoning behind this practice is to allow for a "liminal" experience in an environment where language, food, and customs are strange. Where one's personal resources are stretched to the limit, one often discovers God there at a new depth. This experience has been a powerful maturing one for many of our young Marists. Many of those making *The Spiritual Exercises* often discover, as they look back over their own lives, that God has touched them in such liminal moments in the heart of their own land and own work. I recall such an experience just a few years after I was ordained. I was chaplain to a Catholic tramping (hiking) club, but for this summer vocation they had decided to offer a family outing on a canoe trip down the Wanganui River. This is the longest of New Zealand's rivers, beginning in the middle of the North Island and reaching the sea on the western coast. It can take three to five days, and you may pass through about 120 rapids, depending on the height of the river, which can rise and fall rapidly with the amount of rain in the high country.

I felt some nervousness, because I was not a strong swimmer. My concerns were brushed aside by guarantees that I would be traveling in a large Canadian canoe with experienced crew and that we would all be wearing life jackets constantly. When we arrived at the starting point, I discovered, due to late withdrawals from the expedition, that I ended up in a two-man kayak made of canvas and wood with a young student, also a novice paddler. Over the five days, we ditched in the water four times, the first just thirty meters from the start—much to the amusement of a group of scouts undertaking three-days training before their trip down. The worst moment came in the deep gorge in the middle of the trip. Narrow and dark except for the thin band of sky high above, it was an imposing place, the blackish waters flowing turgidly with the occasional eddying whirlpool a testament to the powerful dynamics deep below. By this time we had come to some terms with our kayak. The sudden appearance of a whirlpool, however, made us both paddle in opposing directions overbalancing the canoe.

Fighting to cling to the upturned hull, I desperately waited for help to pull us to the shore. But the current was strong, the canoes well scattered. My jacket was already sodden, and I was struggling to keep my head out of the water. Despite my best efforts I was swallowing an occasional mouthful. We seemed to drift endlessly with no beach in sight, only vertical walls of shrub and cliff. Just as I felt that my numbed fingers could cling no longer, another canoe came alongside and pulled us to a small grassy shelf. Heaved out of the water, I lay like a beached whale, thanking God for deliverance. Arriving two days later at Pipiriki, where we pulled the canoes from the water, I was still physically conscious of the pull of the water, its sinuous strength, its beauty, but inexorable ruthless power. When I returned to Wellington, where I was teaching, I was shocked to read that one of the scouts who had stood on the bank laughing at us had drowned in an accident coming down the river.

Ecological Reflection

Water is one of the most precious and plentiful resources on this planet. Human bodies are more than 70 percent constituted by water, and we cannot survive more than a few days without drinking. Oceans cover about three-quarters of the globe, and huge reserves of water are stored in the ice fields and glaciers of the poles. Out in mid-Pacific trillions of gallons of seawater are vaporized each day to form the clouds which feed rain bands that irrigate earth's continents. Yet there are areas of the world such as sub-Saharan Africa and parts of the American Southwest where water is becoming a scarce resource. Due to changing weather patterns linked to warming climate and overuse of some aquifers, life in these areas is becoming a more fraught struggle. In the view of some social commentators, just as the struggle for control of oil resources is the hidden engine causing much international turmoil today, in fifty or a hundred years the battle for control of fresh water will be the most likely cause of world conflicts. Water is a key symbol in many religious traditions, so we are not surprised to see it featuring in one of Jesus' great liminal moments as well.

Scripture Reflection: Mk 1:9–11

In those days Jesus came from Nazareth of Galilee and was baptized by John in the Jordan. And just as he was coming up out of the water, he saw the heavens torn apart and the Spirit descending like a dove on him. And a voice came from heaven, "You are my Son, the Beloved; with you I am well pleased."

Scripture Commentary

John the Baptist is a pivotal figure, acting like a hinge between the two Testaments. In many ways he looks back to the Jewish prophets like Elijah. Mark has him dress like the prophet of Carmel (cf. Mk 1:6 and 2 Kgs 1:7–8). Yet in other ways he is a harbinger, pointing to something still over the horizon. His baptism is not a ritual cleansing like the repeated purifications of the Essenes. It is a unique conversion moment in preparation for a new fire that is to sweep the land. When Jesus is baptized, it is the Spirit who provides the testimony that this is the messenger come to inaugurate God's new kingdom. For Jesus himself it must have been a profound ratification of his call, a sense of special bond with God, as it were, a new birth for a new life. Mark underlines this by use of the title "my Son, the Beloved," an unmistakable evoking of the first servant song of Deutero-Isaiah (Is 42:1–9). In this passage we meet the mysterious servant of God who is to represent the chosen people, liberating and leading them, yet being rejected and suffering for them at the same time.

It is also of great significance that Jesus comes to be baptized in the river Jordan. It is the barrier to the promised land that even Moses could not cross. It marks the passage between the place of struggle and learning and the place of settlement. Jesus undergoes this ritual moment of passing across not just for himself, but also for the whole of his people, Israel. Many of the fathers of the church such as Melito of Sardis, Clement of Alexandria, Ephrem, and Philoxenus also saw this event as having a cosmic significance. It would sanctify all water to be a bearer of the Spirit, and it was also a cosmic event marking the beginning of redemption for the universe.

Additional Passages

Is 42:1–9   Here is my servant whom I uphold.
Rom 6:1–14   We are baptized into his death.

Questions for Reflection

1. Can I identify any liminal experiences in my own life? How did they contribute to my sense of identity?
2. What are the moments in my life in which God in various ways has said to me, you are my chosen, my beloved?
3. Do I respect water? Are there ways I could cherish, appreciate and conserve it better?

A Final Thought

O Lord,
One tiny bit of water rests on the palm of my hand.
I bring it to you and with it I bring the whole ocean.
This tiny drop has the power to ease the burning thirst of men,
when spread on the earth,
    to give life to the seed and the future harvest,
when poured on the fire to quench the blaze.
A tiny drop of water
can cleanse the whole of my impurity when
    blessed by your forgiveness.
But, O lord,
more than all this, this tiny drop of water passed over my head
is the symbol of my birth in you.

—Ishpriya

Day 15
Jesus' Temptation and Personal Call

Prayer Desire
I beg God to help me see through the enticements of the evil spirit, whose promises of happiness turn out to be nothing but illusions.

Ignatian Focus
The evil spirit often acts like a false lover. He wants to seduce our hearts while keeping his blandishments and flattery hidden and far from the light of day. (*The Spiritual Exercises* 326)

Introduction
In her 1984 novel, *The Handmaid's Tale,* Margaret Atwood paints a society of oppression and control in which a military elite, behind their austere façade, enjoy a life of pleasure and decadence. In many ways it is a dark reflection of our consumer-driven society. The heroine, working for one of the ruling clique, comes across a glittery woman's magazine from the 1970s or 1980s. With nostalgia she recalls the many small vanities and pleasures that have passed away. But more, she now sees the hollowness at the heart of such publications:

> Though I remembered now. What was in them was promise. They dealt in transformations; they suggested an endless stream of possibilities, extending like the reflections in two mirrors set facing one another, stretching on, replica after replica, to the vanishing point. They suggested one adventure after another, one wardrobe after another, one improvement after another, one man after another. They suggested rejuvenation, pain overcome and transcended, endless love. The real promise in them was immortality. (p. 165)

Atwood captures the myths of the consumer society: the good things will never end; they can be had at no real price; and they will meet the deepest desires of the human heart. When most people reflect critically, they know deep down that these claims are not true. Yet trapped in a world of product branding, in which market research is probing every human frailty and longing, and picking at them with an unflagging barrage of images and logos through TV, billboards, and newsprint, consumers can so easily allow their judgment and will to be submerged and overwhelmed. Numbed by this assault, they turn to a Coke when they want companionship, their Lexus when they want elegance, and a Marlboro when they want freedom.

Ecological Reflection

There are many values of wilderness. It is somewhere to escape from the relentless media pressure of the developed world and the enticements and lies of advertising. It is important to see, nevertheless, that wilderness has two faces. It is national parks and the outback, where you may see no other human face for twenty-four hours or more. But equally it can be a chosen retreat into the wildness within to face one's deepest desires, dreams, and memories away from all television, newspapers, shopping malls, and small talk, long enough to grasp how much they fill the emptiness of our lives. That gives us distance to confront some of the great myths of our day: that everyone is happier today, that they own more, and enjoy more leisure.

These myths are being critiqued by a number of social commentators. It is true that due to computerization and miniaturization the production and availability of material goods has risen greatly over the last twenty years. It is equally clear that more and more of this wealth generated is passing to fewer and fewer hands, so that the gap between rich and poor in global markets grows ever wider. Some of the statistics about huge transnational corporations such as Disney, Nike, and Wal-Mart collected by Kernaghan make sobering reading. That the fifty thousand workers at the Yue Yen factory in China have to work nineteen years to earn what Nike spends on advertising in one year; that in 2000 the Disney CEO Michael Eisner earned $9,783 an hour while Haitian workers earned $.28—at which rate it would take them 16.8 years to earn what he earned in one hour; that in the United States the richest 1 percent of families owned 45 percent of the nation's wealth, up from 20 percent in 1970; that 16.5 percent of people in this great wealthy nation live below the official poverty line, the highest proportion in the developed world. To cap this off, the average worker in the United States in the early 1990s was working annually from 140 to 163 more hours than in the 1970s. We are bombarded by a vast amount of information all around us. Paradoxically this can make it much harder to find the truth that cuts away so much evasion and deception.

Scriptural Reflection: Mt 4:1–11

Then Jesus was led up by the Spirit into the wilderness to be tempted by the devil. He fasted forty days and forty nights, and afterwards he was famished. The tempter came and said to him, "If you are the Son of God, command these stones to become loaves of bread." But he answered, "It is written, 'One does not live by bread alone, but by every word that comes from the mouth of God.'"

Then the devil took him to the holy city and placed him on the pinnacle of the temple, saying to him, "If you are the Son of God, throw yourself down; for it is written, 'He will command his angels concerning you,' and 'On their hands they will bear you up, so that you will not dash your foot against a stone.'" Jesus said to him, "Again it is written, 'Do not put the Lord your God to the test.'"

Again, the devil took him to a very high mountain and showed him all the kingdoms of the world and their splendor; and he said to him, "All these I will give you, if you will fall down and worship me." Jesus said to him, "Away with you, Satan! for it is written, 'Worship the Lord your God, and serve only him.'" Then the devil left him, and suddenly angels came and waited on him.

Scripture Commentary

This a rich passage full of Old Testament allusions and symbolism. First we must note that it is the Holy Spirit that pushes Jesus into the wilderness, for it is not just a fearful place, but also the place of truth and revelation where Moses and Elijah met God face-to-face. Jesus' long fast parallels the preparation time needed by two prophets (cf. Ex 34:18; 1 Kgs 19:8); it also reminds us of the forty years' testing that the Israelites faced before their entry to the promised land.

The first important truth to be learned is that it not God that tempts his people, as the ancient Jews had supposed, but the evil spirit, the deceiver. Second, as Matthew stresses, these are real temptations. Jesus had been called by the Father, but the call was a daunting one.

There were all sorts of competing scenarios for the coming Messiah, among them the military strongman as well as the trickster messiah, beguiling all with wondrous shows, healings, and marvels.

The tests Jesus undergoes correspond to the Jews' three great lapses in the desert: their complaints about the monotony of the manna (Nm 11:4–34), their angry demands for Moses to provide water for them at Massah (Nm 20:1–13), and their bending in adoration before the bronze calf (Ex 32:1–8). We can see a strong link here to the three basic drives that Freud depicted as always being in dynamic tension within each human psyche: the id (or pleasure principle), the superego (seeking self-validation through social approval), and the power of the rampant ego (I alone matter). Without a doubt these same three human drives are at the root of much ecological imbalance and destruction today. These are the roots of human desire, utterly necessary for energy and creativity. But without the moderation and discernment of the Spirit, they turn into cancers, eating away at all that is strong and well-developed in the human psyche. They are the bread and meat of the tempter's standard menu, driving and giving energy to our overconsuming and bloated societies.

Additional Passages
Heb 2:14–18   He wanted to be one just like us.
Lk 4:14–30   Jesus returns to Nazareth and faces rejection.

Questions for Reflection
1. Do I have (or could I create) a place of wilderness where I can go to face my illusions?
2. How could I get to know some people on the margins (poor, sick, unemployed, imprisoned), so as to be exposed to a different picture of the society in which I live?
3. If I were to encounter the same three temptations that Jesus came face-to-face with, what concretely might they look like in my world?

A Final Thought

What I have been preparing to say is this, in wilderness is the preservation of the world. . . . Life consists of wilderness. The most alive is the wildest. Not yet subdued to man, its presence refreshes him. . . . When I would re-create myself, I seek the darkest wood, the thickest and most interminable and to the citizen, most dismal, swamp. I enter as a sacred place, a Sanctum Sanctorum. There is the strength, the marrow, of Nature. In short, all good things are wild and free.

—Henry David Thoreau

Day 16
Jesus Calls His Disciples

Prayer Desire

I entreat God that I may be open to the call of Jesus, inviting me to follow him on the road to Jerusalem.

Ignatian Focus

Christ issues the call "My will is to win the whole world for my Father, to scatter the darkness sown by the evil one, and so enter into my Father's glory. Whoever wishes to accompany me must share the labor with me, so that following me in the suffering, they may also follow me in my glory." (*The Spiritual Exercises* 95)

Introduction

My great-grandfather was an Irish miner who was part of the Linehan party that first discovered gold in Charleston on the west coast of the South Island of New Zealand in 1868. He was just one of the millions of emigrants who quit Ireland in the hundred years between 1780 and 1880 because of huge changes in land use and a string of famines. At the heart of that was the almost total destruction of the potato crop from 1845 to 49 by the blight *plytophera infestans*. The Irish crop was one of just two strains grown in Europe, so that when the disease struck there was nowhere to turn to find a resistant stock. This would come much later with the importation of some the thousands of different stocks still to be found in the Andes and Mexico. God seems to have allowed a vast array of different species and life forms on earth to create a balance that would ensure preservation of some lines even in the worst of famines, diseases, and droughts. Jesus too seems to have called the widest variety of people to be his disciples, to reflect fully the breadth and variety of God's gifts to his people.

Ecological Reflection

Current environmental writing has seen something of a debate on the number of species wiped out by human activity. The number is hard to calculate. Among other factors, we do not know just how many species of living beings, both plant and animal, exist on this planet. Estimates run anywhere between 5 and a 100 million. The bulk of these are insects, and the vast majority are to be found close to the equator in places like Indonesia, Papua New Guinea, and the Amazon basin. Plant species are particularly prodigal in some areas; one small region in Java is famous because about twenty different species of orchids found nowhere else occur over about seven to ten acres. The clear-cutting of the tropical rainforest in Indonesia, the Solomon Islands, and the Amazon has led to the loss of much specialized habitat. Many species can live only in very specific chemical and climatic conditions. With the fragmentation of their habitat, only small islands suitable to their lifestyle may remain, but scattered far from each other, so their numbers soon decline. Many biologists consider that any population that falls below five hundred members is in grave danger of going extinct.

When such loss occurs, we are not aware of the possibilities that have slipped out of our grasp. The discovery of drugs such as aspirin, which was derived from the bark of willow trees by North American Indians, highlights this. Likewise, there is a particular periwinkle from Madagascar that has yielded a drug effective against leukemia. The unforeseen possibilities we discover to make good use of nature point to the unforeseen long-term effects of our destruction of species, both for us in the human sphere and for the whole of the natural world. When we destroy any species, there is a flow-through effect in the diminishment of the food chain and the unchecked surge of former prey. A myriad of other unanticipated effects may wreck ecological havoc in a given area or ecosystem.

While there is a jump from this discussion of the dangers of extinction to the choices we make on how to use the God-given talents we each possess, there is one factor that is constant. It is the impact that one person or a small group can have on our planet. We see this in Jesus' calling of his disciples to mission.

Scripture Reflection: Mt 10:1–8

Then Jesus summoned his twelve disciples and gave them authority over unclean spirits, to cast them out, and to cure every disease and sickness. These are the names of the twelve apostles: first, Simon, also known as Peter, and his brother Andrew; James, son of Zebedee, and his brother John; Philip and Bartholomew; Thomas and Matthew the tax collector; James son of Alphaeus, and Thaddeus; Simon the Cananaean, and Judas Iscariot, the one who betrayed him.

These twelve Jesus sent out with the following instructions: "Go nowhere among the Gentiles, and enter no town of the Samaritans, but rather to the lost sheep of the house of Israel. As you go, proclaim the good news, 'The kingdom of heaven has come near.' Cure the sick, raise the dead, cleanse the lepers, cast out demons. You received without payment; give without payment."

Scripture Commentary

This solemn roll call of the apostles is linked to the powers and mission of the group that is later to emerge as the Christian church. A number of them have already been called individually; here they are commissioned and given power as a group. Jesus is quite unstinting in his demands on them, but prodigal in the powers he extends to them. All that he had done—cures, exorcisms, powerful preaching—they are also to do. He asks no training, exams, supervision, or gradual exposure, just going out and doing what he has done. Breathtaking and innovative as this seems, Jesus also creates a strong link with the past. The stress on the number twelve is clearly a link with the twelve tribes of Israel. Matthew's gospel, of course, depicts Jesus as the new Moses. Matthew views the church as the continuation of the twelve tribes descended from Jacob through Moses. We find the same lists in the other synoptics (Mk 3:16–19, Lk 6:14–26, and Acts 1:13) with just some minor differences, and in almost exactly the same order. Peter always stands first. Yet there is great diversity in the group: Galileans (one from Canaanite territory, and one with a Greek name, Philip), craftsmen, a tax collector, and, from the extreme left of the political spectrum, Simon, a zealot.

Matthew lays emphasis on the Lord's command to go to the Jews and not to Gentiles or the Samaritans. Yet by the time of the Acts of the Apostles (well before Matthew's gospel was written) it is clear that significant changes have occurred. These apostles, whose names are so stressed, have receded to the background, some to seeming extinction. New missionaries are carrying the gospel news—Paul, Silas, Barnabas, Luke—and zealous deacons are active among the Greek-speaking part of the community. There has clearly been a turn to the Gentiles.

Yet when we look closely at the evidence, it is clear that this turn was slow and painful. Even after the sending of the Spirit at Pentecost and Peter's vision about the call of the Gentiles (Acts 10–11:18), it was not really until after the founding of the church at Antioch (Acts 11:20 ff.) that the mission to the Gentiles began in earnest, and then with many a crisis and hiccup. Within this early group, preservation and linking to their Jewish heritage and the faith of Abraham and Moses was seen as a critical badge of unity. All the while a constant evolution and growth of vision was also taking place. This development was embraced when it was seen to be initiated by the Spirit and discerned by the church. Despite its divine call, the church has always been a place of diversity, struggle, and painful resistance to change.

Additional Passages

| Lk 5:1–11 | I will make you fishers of all peoples. |
| 2 Cor 6:4–10 | As ambassadors for Christ we are prepared for both honor and disgrace. |

Questions for Reflection

1. How aware am I of the diverse people who had a part in the faith and love with which I am now gifted?

2. How could I increase my appreciation and encouragement of the diversity of gifts and talents of the faith community in which I worship?
3. What sort of diversity of plants and animals is there in the place that I live? How does that compare with a century ago?

A Final Thought

This is an account of a dream by Moses Cordovero, a sixteenth century Jewish mystic and writer, in which he saw the entire universe as a temple in which the whole of creation sang praise to God:

At every rung of the ladder, extending from the depths of life on earth to the sublimest regions of the spirit, all the elements reach upwards and strive to come ever closer to the holy, divine source of life and blessing. Indeed, in nature there exists a hierarchical order which extends right down to the inorganic elements, differentiated by the measure of the vitality which they receive from the supreme source of the divine light. This sequential connection of the spheres of creation encompasses the mineral, vegetable, animal, and human realms. . . . In this way, the different elements of nature ascend to the threshold of the metaphysical world, where the unfettered human soul will rejoin the heavenly sphere of absolute holiness.

—Moses Cordovero

Day 17
Called to Proclaim New Freedom

Prayer Desire

I beg God to be open to the world of spirits, both good and evil, that pervade the whole of creation.

Ignatian Focus

My desire . . . is for insight into the deceits of the evil leader, and for help to guard myself against them, . . . and into the genuine life which the supreme and truthful commander sets forth, and grace to imitate him. (*The Spiritual Exercises* 139)

Introduction

There is one critical way in which Jesus' time seems to be utterly different from the milieus in which most of us live. In our Western societies dominated by empirical science, unless a reality can be tested, weighed, and measured, or can be arrived at as the result of logical construction or analysis, then it does not exist. In Jesus' world, spirit was seen as a vital dimension of reality. The invisible world of spirit was everywhere, interpenetrating and coexisting with the physical universe. It was populated by a host of beings, angels, cherubim, seraphim, as well as various kinds of evil spirits. In all four gospels Jesus is shown in battle with such evil spirits.

One way that we might understand this vision today comes to us through the work of the American penologist and criminologist Lonnie Athens. Athens grew up in very abusive and violent home, educated himself with great struggles, and then spent many years interviewing particularly violent murderers who had smashed and sliced other humans with apparently no mercy or remorse. What had turned them into such monsters? His discovery was that such men (for they were predominantly male) did not, in the main, suffer from mental disorders or had not lost their freedom because of hereditary factors. All of them conducted a constant dialogue with an inner chorus of models and mentors, often family members or close associates, who had broken down their resistance and initiated them, usually violently, into a world dominated by violence. One can easily imagine how among those inner voices was the voice of the genuinely satanic.

Acceptance of this possibility also begins to shed new light on the old debate about "anthropocentrism," the notion that the entire universe was created for humans and exists primarily for human benefit. Even if there are other intelligent life forms out there in the depths of interstellar space (something many astronomers cautiously accept), it now seems unlikely that that we will find them or they will contact us. That still leaves us with the dilemma of the vast emptiness of the cosmos. Does it exist solely for our benefit? In the piece of creation that we know best, our own planet, it seems that every available ecological niche is taken up by some creature extraordinarily adapted for the climate, food, and chemical environment of that particular opening. It seems quite logical to extend this awareness to a world of spirit that countless humans are convinced that they have touched, seen into, or stumbled across even for just a few moments in their lives. This spiritual world may be filled with a whole spectrum of powers and intelligences that can interact with our world in very specific ways.

Ecological Reflection

In many ways the tyranny of work has alienated many people from a full awareness and embrace of their own humanity and that of people about them. Among others, John Kavanaugh has commented on the "fetishism of commodities," the way in which an obsession with and craving for property and possessions dehumanizes many men and women. The world of material possessions becomes an idol of worship. Just as people can be known by the sort of friends and company they seek, so their self-image is molded by the things they covet. We become like those things we love. When this is something less than human, we are less than human. So it is that, amid a gaping spiritual vacuum, our society is marked by myriad addictions: to television, diets, computers, shopping, cars, work, to name but a few. This is highlighted by contrast with Celtic attitudes to the natural world and work. In the great collection of Celtic songs and prayers known as the *Carmina Gadelica* is a poem entitled "The Consecration of the Seed." Its point is to highlight the likeness between the one who sows the seed and God. Because the sower is in a certain way a priest, a bestower of life, what he does is liturgy as well as labor. His work is also a prayer. Men and women are profoundly linked with the divine in the very process of creation. When they have lost all sense of the divine, they so easily become just users and abusers.

Scripture Reflection: Mk 1:40–45

A leper came to him begging him, and kneeling he said to him, "If you choose, you can make me clean." Moved with pity, Jesus stretched out his hand and touched him, and said to him, "I do choose. Be made clean!" Immediately the leprosy left him, and he was made clean. After sternly warning him he sent him away at once, saying to him, "See that you say nothing to anyone; but go, show yourself to the priest, and offer for your cleansing what Moses commanded, as a testimony to them." But he went out and began to proclaim it freely, and to spread the word, so that Jesus could not go into a town openly, but stayed out in the country; and people came to him from every quarter.

Scripture Commentary

In Mark's gospel, immediately after his encounter with Satan in the wilderness, Jesus sets out to fight against his ancient enemy as he preaches and teaches in Galilee. Mark depicts Jesus' continuing struggle with Satan in four ways. First, by direct exorcism, driving him out of people who had fallen under his sway. Second, by healings. We can note here that the evangelist often depicts the ignorance of the poor as a type of affliction, akin to a disease, that Jesus heals by his teaching. The third area of confrontation with the devil comes in the controversies in which Pharisees and lawyers, and later the priestly class, try to trick and out-argue Jesus so as to destroy his influence over the people. Fourth, Mark particularly underlines the constant struggle Jesus endures because of the obduracy and thickheadedness of his disciples, so slow to understand and slower yet to believe and trust him. Mark clearly sees that all four of these struggles are linked by the devil's plotting and machinations.

The cure of the leper, coming early in Mark's opening chapter, accentuates the evangelist's focus on Satan's opposition to Christ. Jewish thought commonly saw sickness such as leprosy as a punishment for sin. If it was not due to the leper's personal sin, then possibly it was the sin of his family or clan. So sickness and disease were part of the kingdom ruled by the evil spirit. Jesus was also conscious of how so many of the elaborate and costly procedures that the priestly leadership claimed as necessary for a leper to be freed of such contamination were also part of the control mechanisms that the rulers constructed to ensure the dependence of the people on their law. Some manuscripts have another reading of verse 41, "moved with pity." They say, "moved with anger." This is not anger at the leper, but again at the priestly class for their burdensome regulations that made this sick man's fate even worse. In this case it is easier to understand that Jesus' strange command to the leper to go to declare his cure to the priests is heavily ironic. This is what the ex-leper seems to have understood as he went about telling all of his cure. Mark himself underlines this irony by adding the detail about Jesus' growing fame making it impossible for him to enter the cities anymore. That was precisely the law for the leper who was forced to live outside city walls in case of contagion. In taking away the leper's disease, Jesus has accepted his state of isolation.

This story is just the beginning of a whole ministry of healing, teaching, and exorcising in Mark. As Jesus goes about his daily work of ministering to those in need, he is also fighting a war against the hidden spiritual forces that lie behind so many of the evils he meets. His task and the one in which he tries to instruct his disciples is to recognize and drive out the evil spirit and discern and foster the good.

Additional Passages

Mt 14:22–33   Jesus walks on the waters.
Rom 6:10–20   Put on the armor of God's strength.

Questions for Reflection

1. What are my personal inner demons? Can I name them and ask Jesus to free me from them?
2. Am I caught up in the slavery of work and the need to consume? What steps can I take to break these bonds?
3. Can I detect signs in my life that Jesus is inviting me to enroll under his banner, to strive for a world free of sinful addictions and controls?

A Final Thought

Everywhere I go it seems people are killing themselves with work, busyness, rushing, caring and rescuing. Work addiction is a modern epidemic and it is sweeping our land. . . . When work is the sole reservoir for your identity, you are addicted. Work has you, you don't have it.

— Diane Fasel

Day 18
Jesus, Best of Friends

Prayer Desire

I ask humbly for the grace of friendship, to know and walk with Jesus and share his love of his Father's creation.

Ignatian Focus

If you desire to know what type or state of life God is calling you to, keep your eyes fixed on Jesus, who is your friend and model. (*The Spiritual Exercises* 135)

Introduction

Classic writings on friendship have highlighted four different modes of being friends. The first is affective love and support; such a friend is always loyal, uncritical, and readily praises. The second sort is much more linked to common activities; it covers people who delight in sailing a yacht or playing cards together. The third variety is more based on intellectual sharing; such friends enjoy sharing ideas and new discoveries, reading the same books or going to films together to discuss them afterward. Fourth, we have the loyal critic, one who points out possible flaws in our personal or professional behavior that need to be addressed, for example, a business mentor or personal tutor. It is possible to find all four facets in the same person, but it is much more common for a particular friend to represent one of these dimensions strongly and the other three to lesser extents.

Friendship is of immense importance to our sense of personal development and worth. Psychological studies show that once a person has enough wealth and possessions to ensure personal freedom and relative security from want, the level of subsequent possessions is of much less account for many people. Individuals of the same social stratum have expressed similar satisfaction with life in countries whose wealth levels are as diverse as those of the United States, Brazil, India, and Israel. Asked if they had achieved the American dream yet, 5 percent of those earning less than $15,000 a year thought so while 6 percent of those earning over $45,000 gave exactly the same answer. What emerges is that happiness does not relate closely to one's level of earnings as much as to family life (especially marriage), then to work, and the leisure to develop talents and friendship. Friendship is especially significant because for many this is one of the highest values of married life. Friendship opens up not just the possibility of new areas of relationship, but also new horizons of discovery and fulfillment. That is why it is such an important insight when retreatants come to see that Jesus wants to share a deep and abiding friendship with them.

Ecological Reflection

Faced with ecological degradation in parts of the world, a number of writers have begun to see companionship or even friendship with nature as a way of revisioning our relationship with the natural world. This is not an effort to treat animals or plants in a sentimental or overly romantic way. Rather, it is in part an effort to discover new theological bases to express the proper relationship between humans, animals, or trees.

A starting point for this viewpoint is to reexamine the very common patristic notion of Christ as the second Adam. Maximus the Confessor, for instance, saw this relationship in terms of mediation. When the first Adam was still fully graced and integral, the animals obeyed him. At this time, Adam could read their inmost beings (he had named them) and was in total harmony with them, seeing their inner logic and beauty. After the fall, such a relationship could be partly restored through grace. We see this reflected in the lives of some of the desert fathers such as on the occasion when Paul and Anthony met in a desolate place and a crow brought them a loaf of bread. Then there is the story of Abbot Gerasimus, who had removed a thorn from a savage lion's paw. After his death the lion sought out his grave, and lay there roaring from grief until its own death. We find the same insight in some of the legends from Celtic spirituality such as St. Columban in the Vosges Mountains. When he walked, animals would come at his call. He would stroke and caress them, and even the squirrels would run in and out of his cowl. Then there is the image of St. Kevin and the blackbird, which is still seen in many rural settings in Ireland. When praying one day, he had his arms extended out of the window of his tiny cabin. So still was he in prayer that a mother black-bird laid her eggs there. So the saint stayed in that posture of prayer until all the chicks were fully hatched.

Alongside of these popular stories we find another historical practice critical to the Catholic tradition. That is the trend of taking pagan myths and symbols and baptizing and reinterpreting them in Christian ways. Early Christians took the beasts of Greek and Roman mythology, such as the centaur, the griffin, the hippocampus, and the hippogriff, and attached Christian symbolism and meaning to the images. The figure of Orpheus was pushed into service as Christ the good shepherd in murals and frescoes. The fourth-century *Commentary if Physiologus* (attributed to St. Epiphanius) contains twenty-six chapters dedicated just to animals and had wide impact over the next five centuries, being the basis for many of the Christian bestiaries that were hugely popular in the Middle Ages. Many illustrated ancient Christian manuscripts contained animals and birds in the margins. Simon Schama's *Landscape and Memory* traces the way in which Christian artists used images taken from pagan tree worship, smuggled in biblical ideas such as the tree of life, the tree of Calvary, and the vine and the branches, to end up with extraordinary works such as Taddeo Gaddi's *The Tree of the Cross* (mid-fourteenth century) and Jacques Callot's etching the *Tree of St. Francis* (ca. 1620). Let us now return to the Christian scriptures to see how this theme of companionship and friendship became so central in Christian thought.

Scripture Reflection: Lk 10:38–42

Now as they went on their way, he entered a certain village, where a woman named Martha welcomed him into her home. She had a sister named Mary, who sat at the Lord's feet and listened to what he was saying. But Martha was distracted by her many tasks; so she came to him and asked, "Lord, do you not care that my sister has left me to do all the work by myself? Tell her then to help me." But the Lord answered her, "Martha, Martha, you are worried and distracted by many things; there is need of only one thing. Mary has chosen the better part, which will not be taken away from her."

Scripture Commentary

This short Lucan story operates on two levels. On the first, it is a story of sibling tensions and resentment. Its background is a close friendship between Jesus, two sisters, Mary and Martha, and their brother Lazarus, who lived at Bethany, a short distance from Jerusalem. Martha, seemingly the older, is conscious of her role of hospitality, a sacred task in Jewish etiquette, and the importance of their guest. Her way of showing love is practical, what we sometimes call "fussing over." Aware that her younger sister is totally absorbing Jesus' attention, she feels neglected and undervalued so tries to get Jesus to take her side. Not only does Jesus refuse to play along with this strategy; he also tells Martha that there are times when listening and sharing are the most important part of friendship.

On another level, this passage tells us a lot about the church for which Luke was writing, a mainly gentile church, scattered throughout Asia Minor. There it was women who often hosted the local church in their homes, and it was in their houses that the eucharist was celebrated. This was a break from Judaism, in which women were devotees and supporters of particular rabbis but not their disciples. By contrast, Mary's stance of sitting and listening at the Master's knees is traditionally the role of the disciple. Also the Greek word that Martha uses for "serving" is the same word that is used for Jesus' presiding at table fellowship during the many meals recorded in Luke's gospel. In the story Jesus begins as guest but through his words becomes the dominant host and teacher. Mary teaches us that Jesus is a precious friend, but also provider, host, and the food itself.

Additional Passages

Jn 4:1–42   Jesus and the Samaritan woman.
Phil 1:3–11   I thank God whenever I remember you.

Questions for Reflection

1. With whom do I share the gift of friendship? Am I grateful for what such friendship brings?
2. Do I ever see the image of Christ in the world of nature? How could I develop this gift more?

3. What do my relationships with animals tell me of my inner harmony or lack of it?

A Final Thought

O God, I thank thee
for all the creatures thou hast made,
so perfect in their kind—
great animals like the elephant and the rhinoceros,
humorous animals like the camel and the monkey,
friendly ones like the dog and the cat,
working ones like the horse and the ox,
timid ones like the squirrel and the rabbit,
majestic ones like the lion and the tiger,
for birds with their songs.
O Lord, give us such love for thy creation,
that love may cast out fear,
and all thy creatures see in man
their priest and friend
through Jesus Christ our Lord.

— George Appleton

Day 19:
Jesus, Man of the Land

Prayer Desire

I ask God for the gift of caring for the world and all in it and also ask that I might understand what that might mean for me.

Ignatian Focus

Among those whom God calls will be some with great generosity of heart and spirit who will want to give themselves completely to God even if this means poverty and personal sacrifice. (*The Spiritual Exercises* 97)

Introduction

Jesus was himself a craftsman and came from a small rural village; he lived in easy communion with the land. Key events such as his birth, temptation, and sermons on the mountain and seashore are in rural settings. They were favored places for his own prayer and reflection (Mt 14:23, 17:1; Mk 6:46). Much of his teaching is filled with images of seeds, vines, shepherds, lilies, birds, and foxes. He used natural materials like clay and spittle in his miracles and represented himself under the symbols of water (Jn 4:13–14), bread (Jn 6:18), and light (Jn 8:12). At the end of his life he endured anguish in a garden, was executed on a hillside, was buried in a garden, and made his first risen appearance there.

Many devout Jews expected that one of the Messiah's chief roles would be to free *herez Israel,* the land of Israel. The land was their covenant inheritance, the special place of God's presence and action. Its very soil was sacred, steeped with the blood of prophets and warriors who had died to protect it. Now it groaned under the impious practices of the Roman invaders. Jesus' agenda could not be confined by such nationalistic dreams, however. We have seen that right from the infancy narratives, the synoptic writings are full of hints that Jesus' gospel was far wider than just Israel. At the start of his gospel John depicts Jesus as cleansing the temple (Jn 2:13–22). He foretells that it would cease to be the symbol of God's presence among his people; instead his risen body would be the new temple. Similarly, as the news of the gospel spread through the towns and cities of Asia Minor and then the Mediterranean region, it became clear that Christians owed an allegiance to something higher than their native land. Jesus himself was the new temple but also the new promised land.

Ecological Reflection

To have an ecological vision of this world is to be aware how humble the human role is. Even the age of our species should alert us to this fact. One image used by Richard Overman compares the history of our planet to an anthology of ten volumes, each page representing a million years. Each volume consists of five hundred pages. On this basis, cellular life appears in the eighth volume, and it is only on page 465 that birds and warm-blooded animals supersede the reptiles. As for humans, we make our first appearance on page 499 of the final volume. The period of civilization from about 4000 B.C. onward is represented by the last two words on the final page. In wondering how humans relate to this world, we might do worse than to ponder on the link between the biblical image of dominion in Gn 1:26 and the term *dominus* (Lord) used in the Vulgate translation of the Bible. As all humans are made in the image of Christ, so we are masters as Jesus was, not as one who dominates but as one who serves. Therefore sacrificial self-giving is the correct moral stance for humans in this world. That is not to belittle human uniqueness and dignity. Niles Eldredge in his work on the importance of biodiversity points out that microbes of which we are usually totally unaware, and insects which we often fear and avoid, are critical for the very continuance of human life on this planet. With regard to both of them, he quotes a biological version of the law of inverse proportions: "The less conspicuous a group of organisms may be, the more it usually turns out to be at the very center of things." What could be truer of our very late and very insignificant place in the gradual unfolding of our universe?

We have already reflected on the importance of wilderness for men and women. It reminds them of their status in belonging to a nature that is far greater than their narrow desires and dreaming. Yet when we come to our role with regard to this planet, it may be that the image of gardening is more crucial for us as a species. We share this planet with a myriad of other life forms, on whom we depend and which we must cultivate, contain, and occasionally control for our health and survival. Gardening is such an exercise in management, but it also requires knowledge of and respect for the plants we are trying to nurture or else our garden just dies.

We should not therefore be surprised to discover that the image of gardening has been frequently used in Christian writings. In the fourth century St. Macarius used it as a picture for the purifying of the soul. The image was applied to monastic life by St. Benedict. This was very apt, because so many of his new foundations were in what would later be Bohemia, Hungary, and Poland, places where the monks labored to drain marshes, plant crops, and grow orchards. It was the image favored by mystics as diverse as St. Maximus, John of the Cross, Gerrard Winstanley, and Roger Crab.

In one of his addresses Gregory Nazianzus points out the good deeds that should flow from such a model. Since all the natural goods that we possess—rain, agriculture, food, crafts, and especially human dominion over the rest of nature—are gifts from God, then we are bound as images of God to show similar kindness and love. Christians in particular should not accumulate goods while others are in want. "Let us by no means be wicked stewards of God's gifts to us. . . . While others suffer poverty, let us not labor to hoard and pile up money," Gregory says. Since God pours down his gifts indiscriminately on both just and sinners, and makes the sun shine on all the earth, then Christians are also obliged to ensure that these common goods are available to all peoples too. Jesus, the man of the land, shared this outlook—something we see in the following parable from Luke.

Scripture Reflection: Lk 16:19–31

"There was a rich man who was dressed in purple and fine linen and who feasted sumptuously every day. And at his gate lay a poor man named Lazarus, covered with sores, who longed to satisfy his hunger with what fell from the rich man's table; even the dogs would come and lick his sores. The poor man died and was carried away by the angels to be with Abraham. The rich man also died and was buried. In Hades, where he was being tormented, he looked up and saw Abraham far away with Lazarus by his side. He called out, 'Father Abraham, have mercy on me, and send Lazarus to dip the tip of his finger in water and cool my tongue; for I am in agony in these flames.' But Abraham said, 'Child, remember that during your lifetime you received your good things, and Lazarus in like manner evil things; but now he is comforted here, and you are in agony. Besides all this, between you and us a great chasm has been fixed, so that those who might want to pass from here to you cannot do so, and no one can cross from there to us.' He said, Then, father, I beg you to send him to my father's house—for I have five brothers—that he may warn them, so that they will not also come into this place of torment.' Abraham replied, 'They have Moses and the prophets; they should listen to them.' He said, 'No, father Abraham; but if someone goes to them from the dead, they will repent.' He said to them, 'If they do not listen to Moses and the prophets, neither will they be convinced even if someone rises from the dead.'"

Scripture Commentary

In its context in Luke this story is clearly an urgent summons to repentance and conversion. Yet as we look at the first six verses, it is not immediately evident what crime the rich man had committed to merit the fire of Hades. We certainly do not hear Lazarus accusing him of any injustice or exulting at his fate. Only as we reflect on the very different outcome of their lives do we come to see that the rich man's failure is precisely that he did not do anything at all. He seemed utterly oblivious to this thing lying at his gate, failing to see their common humanity and the bond that linked them across the divide of wealth. The story completely bypasses Lazarus's moral character to stress Dives's indifference and the irreversibility of his condemnation. Despite his pleading words, he has to face up to the gospel reality that it is deeds, not words, that measure the worth of life, and that his deeds were profoundly self-centered and callous. The last two verses contain another trenchant judgment. Rising from the dead is clearly an allusion to Jesus' resurrection, and there are those who will not accept it even as Luke writes. The question that the evangelist leaves hanging in the air is, Will the five brothers and all who hear this parable change their lifestyle to care for those in need?

Additional Passages

Mt 13:44–46   The treasure in the field.

Lk 11:1–13   Jesus teaches about prayer.

Questions for Reflection

1. Who owns the land and grows the food in the area in which I live? How could I find this out?

2. Are there people like Lazarus close to where I work, sitting unnoticed at the gate or on the streets? Who cares what becomes of them?
3. Is there any piece of land that is sacred to me, that evokes ties of family, history, and origins?

A Final Thought

When a farmer sets out to till the ground he has to take proper tools and clothing for work in the fields; so when Christ, the heavenly king and true husbandman, came to humanity laid waste by sin, he clothed himself in a body and carried the cross as his implement and cultivated the deserted soul. He pulled up the thorns and this-tles of evil spirits and tore up the weeds of sin. With fire he burnt up all the harvest of its sins. When thus he had tilled the ground of the soul with the wooden plough of his cross, he planted in it a love-ly garden of the Spirit; a garden which brings forth for God as its master the sweetest and most delightful fruits of every sort.

—From a homily attributed to St. Macarius

Day 20
Jesus, Transfigured on the Mountain

Prayer Desire

I pray that I may see how God is transfiguring my inner being, and I long for this to blossom even further.

Ignatian Focus

If God allows me to experience a time of poverty, I should not fear it but embrace it deeply so that in this experience I may draw near-er to Jesus who became poor for my sake. (*The Spiritual Exercises* 157)

Introduction

The fullest biography of Thomas Merton, the Cistercian monk, mys-tic, and social critic, is Michael Mott's *The Seven Mountains of Thomas*

Merton. One of his themes is the paradox between the monk fixed by vow to his monastery and the global twentieth-century nomad that Merton was. Born in Prades, France, near the border with Spain, Merton's father was a New Zealander and his mother an American artist. Raised mainly in England, he went to the United States as an undergraduate and remained there until his final journey in 1968, when he went to Thailand to attend an international conference on Marxism and monasticism. There he died accidentally as the result of an electric shock.

Late in his life, Merton reflected much on his world geography and made sense of his life with an image he seems to have taken from Dante's *Purgatory,* where the mountain is the place of final illumination. Merton saw his own life linked to seven mountains, from Mt. Canijou, which dominated Prades, to Mt. Kanchenjunga in Darjeeling. Attending a conference there before moving on to Thailand, Merton awoke after some cloudy days to find the mountain filling the sky outside his window. Stirred by a profound insight, he scribbled in his diary, "The full beauty of the mountain is not seen until you too consent to the impossible paradox: it is and it is not. When nothing more needs to be said, the smoke of ideas clears, the mountain is SEEN."

Before setting out on his final journey, Merton had mentioned to one of his friends that he was looking at the possibility of returning home by way of New Zealand so that he could see where his father was born and meet a few of his relatives who still lived there. Had he ever made it to Christchurch, he might have experienced a strange sense of déjà vu. Christchurch is a small and sedate city, very English in its design and atmosphere, with the Avon River winding its gentle way around streets called Leicester, St. Albans, Rugby, St. Asaph, Oxford, Peterborough, and such. Yet dominating the southeast of the city stand the Port Hills, thrusting out of the ancient floodplain. When you climb the long road to the summit, there over the lip is a deep natural harbor, the drowned caldera of an ancient volcano. And if you drive a little more south and east, you climb over into the superb port of Akaroa and realize that the whole of this Banks Peninsula is a sleeping volcano, the remains of a series of once spectacular eruptions. Merton would have known that another mountain had overlooked his father's life and destiny.

Ecological Reflection

The Wanganui River makes its way to the sea at the small city of Wanganui. Not too far north of here stands the lone peak of Mt. Taranaki, its almost perfectly symmetrical volcanic cone surveying the sea below and the thousands of acres of lush farmland that it has helped to create on its other three sides. Mountains in New Zealand are spiritual and holy places for the Maori, as they are for many indigenous peoples. They are the dwelling place of the guardian spirits. In Maori mythology, Taranaki was once a god who dwelt with the other great peaks, Tongariro, Ngauruhoe, and Ruapehu in the central volcanic plateau of the North Island. Tongariro was married to the beautiful Pihanga, but was coveted by Taranaki, who attempted to seduce her. A fierce war broke out between the mountains. Tongariro triumphed and Taranaki fled in grief and anger to the sea. His track to the sea was the deep gorge which was filled with water poured out by Tongariro as an effort to heal the rift—and so the Wanganui was born.

This story is a powerful reminder to us that there are sacred places in all religions—mountains, rivers, bridges—where the presence of the sacred is felt to be close. Two great religious traditions met in one of these places when Jesus experienced his moment of transfiguration on Mt. Tabor.

Scripture Reflection: Lk 9:28–36

Now about eight days after these sayings Jesus took with him Peter and John and James, and went up on the mountain to pray. And while he was praying, the appearance of his face changed, and his clothes became dazzling white. Suddenly they saw two men, Moses and Elijah, talking to him. They appeared in glory and were speaking of his departure, which he was about to accomplish at Jerusalem. Now Peter and his companions were weighed down with sleep; but since they had stayed awake, they saw his glory and the two men who stood with him. Just as they were leaving him, Peter said to Jesus, "Master, it is good for us to be here; let us make three dwellings, one for you, one for Moses, and one for Elijah"—not knowing what he said. While he was saying this, a cloud came and overshadowed them; and they were terrified as they entered the cloud. Then from the cloud came a voice that said, "This is my Son, my Chosen; listen to him!" When the voice had spoken, Jesus was found alone. And they kept silent and in those days told no one any of the things they had seen.

Scripture Commentary

We cannot understand this passage without looking back to "these sayings" referred to in verse 28. That is the account of Peter's acknowledgment that Jesus is the Christ, the Messiah who is to come, and of Jesus' insistence that his fate is be rejected, suffer, and die before rising again. Needless to say, this is a huge shock to the disciples, especially to Peter. In Mark's account of this incident, when Peter tries to dissuade Jesus from such an outcome he is severely rebuked by Jesus (Mk 8:32–33).

The brilliance associated with Jesus' face alerts us that we are entering into one of the experiences of the numinous that we find in the Jewish scriptures. The mountain setting recalls to us the manifestations of God that came to Moses and Elijah on Mt. Horeb. When the three of them speak of his imminent departure, it is easy to see from the previous conversation that it is Jesus' suffering, death, and glorification that is being spoken about, especially since both Moses and Elijah were themselves rejected prophets. Luke stresses that what is to happen has already been chosen by God, a theme he will reiterate when the risen Jesus meets the disciples on the road to Emmaus (Lk 24:26–27).

The mention by Peter of three dwellings would alert all Jewish readers to the feast of booths or tabernacles. This was perhaps the greatest of the three major feasts in the time of Jesus, the others being Passover and Pentecost. It took the form of thanksgiving at harvest time. There was a procession bearing pomegranates and grapes, and the people slept outside in small booths made of boughs during the octave of the feast. Its purpose was to stress the future final reign of God in the world and in history. As in the appearances of God at Mt. Horeb, the enveloping cloud is a sign of the divine presence. Though terrified, Peter wants to prolong this experience, for it seems to give him the illusion of controlling what is happening in his life. But the voice that at his baptism could be heard only by Jesus now addresses the disciples too. On the way down from the mountain, Jesus interprets the full meaning of the admonition "listen to him," telling them that they in their turn will be asked to follow him in his departure to the Father through death at the hands of their own people. The disciples' reaction is to be totally overwhelmed and silent. In the face of this revelation on the mountain there is nothing that can be said.

Additional Passages

Jn 11:1–45   The raising of Lazarus.

Mt 26:6–13   Jesus is anointed.

Questions for Reflection

1. Have you ever been on a mountain? What were your reactions and feelings?
2. Have you witnessed moments of transfiguration in your own or friends' lives? What brought them about?
3. Are you able to entrust your own passage into death into God's hands? Is there anything that is holding you back?

A Final Thought

All things are said to be transfigured in the transfiguration of Christ in as far as something of each creature was transfigured in Christ. For in his human nature, Christ has something in common with all creatures. With the stone he shares existence; with plants he shares life; with animals, he shares sensation; and with the angels, he shares intelligence. Therefore, all things are said to be transformed in Christ since, by virtue of his humanity, he embraces something of every creature in himself when he is transfigured."

—St. Bonaventure

Week 3 *hree*

DEATH TO ILLUSION

In Week Two of the Exercises some of the joy of the journey comes simply from being on the road with Jesus. Many of us live pretty constrained existences: long work hours, many meetings, tight timetables and expectations. On the road with Jesus one never knows what is coming next. Sometimes it is an old woman bent over with arthritis and the shame of being shunned. On another occasion it is feuding with a talented but arrogant young lawyer itching to take down a peg or two this wild prophet from the provinces. There are tears and the cut and thrust of debate—all the color and companionship of the highway and the back roads.

In Week Three the journeys get progressively shorter. From Bethany to Jerusalem to prepare for the paschal supper (Mt 26:17–25); from the upper room to the Mount of Olives (Lk 22:39–46); from there to the high priest's house (Mk 14:54–63), and the Sanhedrin (Lk 22:66–71), then on to Pilate (Lk 23:1–7) and Herod (Lk 23:6–12); then the final journey to the hill of Golgotha (Lk 23:26–33). At each step the group of Jesus' friends and supporters shrinks; the crowd of his accusers and torturers grows. When his inner turmoil is at its peak in the Garden of Gethsemane, his three closest friends are nearby, but half asleep. In the inner court of the high priest only Peter remains, vehemently rejecting any connection with him (Lk 22:54–62). Under the cross all have fled, except perhaps John, and a few women who loved him most, including his mother (Jn 19:25–27). We move from the candlelit brilliance of the upper room to the shadows of the Garden at Gethsemane, to the flickering firelight of Caiaphas's court, to the blackness of the execution cell under the praetorium, and last of all to the unnatural gloom shrouding Golgotha.

Many retreatants feel great reluctance as they begin to move into this final journey with Jesus. This is caused partly by tiredness. Dramatic swings of emotion, the discovery and growth of new identity, and long hours of prayer begin to drain reserves of energy. When new life and vision have flowered (sometimes too the stirrings of a new career or apostolate) there is an instinctive recoil when the figure of death is known to be waiting around the next corner. One is also entering a zone of great personal danger. What one is embarking on is a voyage of cultural suicide, a challenge to the most enduring myths that power the dynamics of our entire Western culture and civilization: that personal happiness is the fruit won by busyness, usefulness, and an unrelenting belief in success. Jesus' death stands in total opposition to each of these slogans. That is why Ignatius urges each retreatant to seek out Christ, stay with him and beg his aid in entering this painful place: "Then I will begin with great effort to strive to grieve, be sad, and weep. In this way I will labor through all the points that follow"(*The Spiritual Exercises* 195).

It is a time of silence. Not just the exterior quiet that has been the norm for the first two weeks but also an interior quiet. It is not a time for the inward music of the imagination or for making the imaginative leaps and journeys that marked the first two weeks. The meditations themselves are unrelieved. Ignatius proposes no other exercises but praying the gospel passages. He encourages the retreatants to apply their senses avidly to each scene. Each incident of the passion is to be lived through individually. Though there is a great deal of material in the passion narratives, Ignatius exhorts the one making the retreat not to try to push through it all but to stay in depth with particular incidents until what they have to reveal has been exhausted. Then the journey is taken again, this time in one step, often on a wilderness day that the retreatant will spend alone, perhaps in the hills, with just simple requirements for food and a text of perhaps Mark's passion account in a day pack.

Walking the way of the cross may lead the retreatant to want to help bear the burden of discipleship. Sometimes such a desire can be built on a false and tyrannical picture of a demanding and vindictive God. For the bulk of those making the Exercises any such distorted image should have been identified and purified by the conversion processes of the initial weeks. Without this they cannot enter the reality of the passion fruitfully, and Ignatius accepted that some of those who have followed the Exercises to this point will not yet be ready to make the next step—Week Three. Even among those who are ready to move forward there may still be vestiges of self-contempt and punishment, the legacy of many years of self-depreciation. This will show up in deeply entrenched attitudes such as "the more you suffer, the more you will be like Christ," leading to choices to make life as burdensome as possible. For such people, penetrating the inner meaning of Jesus' death will not be possible, because they have already constructed a rigid picture of the sort of following that God will ask of them (cf. Mt 13:13–17). Such stances are utterly at odds with the freedom and joy that Christ promised would be the mark of his followers. They also ignore the fact that continual suffering destroys most people, rather than saving them. The goal of the Exercises is liberation, not subjugation.

As in the previous two weeks, at this time too the character of their relationship with Jesus changes subtly for people making the Exercises. Accompanying Jesus as his friend, I must strive simply to be there for him, watching with him, begging him to help me enter and comprehend every moment of his suffering. For many retreatants, there is a call for a subtle but crucial change: from companionship to union, from sympathy to suffering with. For many, the hardest struggle is to trust, to be able to abandon themselves totally into God's hands as Jesus did. Whereas insight, imagination, and new perspectives brought great consolation in the first weeks, now just being there with Jesus is enough.

Another common struggle for retreatants is the tendency to focus on one's personal pain and discomfort at the indignities and degradation that are the subjects of constant reflection, rather than on the pain and inner desolation of Jesus, who endured them. For some personalities, simply being beside Jesus as he goes through this is unbearable; they have an overwhelming impulse to protect him from this pain, or

they want to take it on themselves. People commonly use three unconscious defense mechanisms to escape their unbearable discomfort. The
first is to lose themselves in details: what color, height, shape, and texture was the pillar to which Jesus was tied to be scourged? The second
is to drift into seminumb inattentiveness. And the third is to make their
meditations like TV soap operas, full of tears and powerful emotions
but all switched off when the show finishes. It is critical for anyone
tempted to such strategies to comprehend the reasons for Jesus' sorrow
and grief rather than to consider any action they can take to curtail the
pain. That is why a persistent theme of prayer must be asking Christ to
free us from *our* feelings so as to be with *his* feelings. For this is the time
when Jesus reaches out to beg for the retreatant's support, to be alongside him as he suffers. To persist here means seeing through many
temptations. One such subtle temptation in contemplating the immensity of Jesus' sorrows is to write off one's own troubles as quite insignificant and thus become resigned to mediocrity.

Another source of intense discomfort arises from the way in which
Jesus' suffering puts us in contact with the sorrow of the world, all the
violence, innocent suffering, intimate betrayals, and civil corruption
that occur in every society. Accepting this brokenness, it is so easy to
feel utterly discouraged and helpless in the face of the need for continuing hope. Touching the fragility of the limits can also elicit sudden
strong feelings from the retreatant's unconscious. Powerful sexual longings and a sense of sexual vulnerability are not uncommon.
Temptations to hopelessness in the face of death's all-conquering presence are not unknown. At such moments, retreatants can also know
loneliness at a depth they never dreamed possible. This is when it is
good to recall that the price is high because the gift to be gained is
priceless. In this connection Dorothy Day commented, "Neither revo-
lutions nor faith is won without keen suffering. For me Christ was not
to be bought for thirty pieces of silver but with my heart's blood. We
do not buy cheap in this market."

Day 21
Last Supper—Betrayal and Desertion

Prayer Desire

I ask the grace to accept that betrayal and desertion may be the price of loving—yet also to accept that love is worth that risk.

Ignatian Focus

I ask to know grief with Christ grieving, heartbreak with Christ heartbroken, weeping, inward pain over the great pain that Christ suffered for me. (*The Spiritual Exercises* 203)

Introduction

One of our unique characteristics as human beings is the way that we shape the world around us to our needs and wants. We are creatures of our environment, yet we are constantly modifying our landscape, our homes, our clothes, and now through biogenetics, even our live-stock and our own bodies. This freedom to shape the earth is limited only by the physical and chemical laws of our universe. Nevertheless, we live in a world that is subject to the interplay of chance and neces-sity; some things we can change, while other things change us, some-times totally. In such a world we cannot depict God simply as the one who ensures order. The randomness and chaos of our lives flows part-ly from the fact that God has relinquished control over all that happens. This does not mean that he has abdicated his love or rule, but simply that he has chosen to achieve redemption from within creation rather than working like a puppeteer high above the stage, unseen but actual-ly pulling all the strings. God even made himself subject to rejection and suffering by choosing to create a world marked by freedom and randomness, and even more by choosing to live in that world as a human being.

The pain that can come from living in such a world is already pres-ent in the creation story. First of all, Adam was lonely and felt incom-plete; he needed Eve to feel whole and to share his life with. Both Adam and Eve were limited. Like all humans, they were not big enough, strong enough, or smart enough to do everything. In the creation story this is symbolized by the tree of the knowledge of good and evil and the limits it imposes. Being incomplete, all humans are dependent on others for many needs. We are interdependent in the sense that we exist only to the extent that we "suffer" the existence of others. This includes not just other humans, but also other animals and natural objects such as trees, rocks, and soil. But this mutual dependence also requires the cooperation and love of others, giving us the chance not just to live but also to flourish. Even in paradise humans were tempted; they were subject to anxiety. Eve did not know what the morrow would bring and perhaps wanted to free herself of the burden of trust in God's providence (far better to know what is going to happen yourself). Just being created means being limited, with the ability to go wrong and sin. On the other hand, it is precisely these limitations that are the source of so many of our joys. For instance, without loneliness we would not know the sweetness of friendship; without limits we would have no challenges and peaks to climb or unexpected surprises; without temptation the moral life with its struggle and elation over freedom won would not exist. Finally, without anxiety we would never experience the comfort of joy and relief when our worst fears are resolved. Without anxiety we would be shallow people, devoid of the passion and feeling that comes from waiting long or facing the loss of all in achieving our deepest dreams.

Jesus experienced agony in the garden because he had embraced such a world. He had labored to share his vision, his call, and even some of his powers with the disciples. At the Last Supper he gave them the ultimate gift, his very life—body and blood—in the form of bread and wine. One does not make a last will and testament without accepting the reality of death. Part of the agony in the garden was his acceptance that the disciples were going to run from that gift. The rejection was as concrete and painful as Judas's kiss and hollow words. It included the incomprehension and cowardice of the disciples, and Peter's brash overconfidence. But most painful would have been the sense of desertion by his Father. At the moment when his struggle with Satan was to reach its pinnacle, when the powers of darkness, hatred, and death were to prevail, when he most needed the support and power of the Father who had called him, at this moment the Father had vanished also.

Ecological Reflection

Many people find it easy and pleasant to focus on the beauty, harmony, and order of nature, say, in a field of sunflowers all holding their heads up toward the sun that bathes and feeds them. The truth of our universe, however, is that it is also a violent place, full of death and destruction. There are two reasons underlying such violence. The first is the sheer magnitude of the forces involved. Take as an example the eruption of Mt. Taupo in the central North Island of New Zealand that formed Lake Taupo in A.D. 186. It was probably the most powerful explosion of the last seven thousand years on earth, the fierce red sunsets it caused were noted by chroniclers in both China and Rome. It blasted out a hundred cubic kilometers of ash and debris, the plume reaching fifty kilometers into the atmosphere. The superb trout-fishing lake enjoyed by tourists today is the result of the 616-square-kilometer caldera, with a bottom so deep that it has still not been successfully mapped.

The second factor underlying the violence of nature is that all higher forms of life are part of a web of life, living from and off one another. Most humans stand astride a mountain of sheep, cattle, pigs, fish, chicken, and other fowl that have died so that they might live; not to mention the acres of grass, cereals, and vegetable crops that have been needed to fatten these animals. To see nature as it truly is, we need to acknowledge its darker side. The langur monkeys of the Himalaya are a good example. They move in herds of one breeding male with about seventy consorts. When a male is strong enough to drive away the previous king of the harem, his first tactic is to start killing the baby langurs, despite the efforts of the mothers to stop him. A few days after the death of her babies, the female will come into heat again. In seven months all the babies in the herd carry the new king's genes. Nature is full of such rawness.

When we are able to look nature in the face, with all her moods and states, then we humans are free to acknowledge that we do not control this world or the universe. We are short-term tenants, here on trust, not knowing how long our tenure is to be. We are cosmic orphans, and being prone to desertion and betrayal is part of who we are. Even Jesus himself had to take the full weight of that in the upper room and in the Garden of Gethsemane.

Scripture Reflection: Mt 26:26–35

While they were eating, Jesus took a loaf of bread, and after bless-ing it he broke it, gave it to his disciples, and said, "Take, eat; this is my body." Then he took a cup, and after giving thanks he gave it to them, saying, "Drink from it, all of you; for this is my blood of the covenant, which is poured out for many for the forgiveness of sins. I tell you, I will never again drink of this fruit of the vine until that day when I drink it new with you in my Father's kingdom."

When they had sung the hymn, they went out to the Mount of Olives.

Then Jesus said to them, "You will all become deserters because of me this night; for it is written, 'I will strike the shepherd, and the sheep of the flock will be scattered.' But after I am raised up, I will go ahead of you to Galilee." Peter said to him, "Though all become deserters because of you, I will never desert you." Jesus said to him, "Truly I tell you, this very night, before the cock crows, you will deny me three times." Peter said to him, "Even though I must die with you, I will not deny you." And so said all the disciples.

Scripture Commentary

In many ways Jesus' struggle in the Garden of Gethsemane is the concluding bout of the battle between himself and Satan that began with his temptations after his baptism. The nub of the agony is that Jesus knows that he has to surrender; he must, as it were, yield the bat-tleground to the enemy to return as conqueror. The mystery here is wrapped in the New Testament word *paradidonai*, "handed over." Not only is it used of Judas's betrayal, but it becomes a key word for Jesus' surrender of himself for the salvation of the world (see Jn 3:16 and Rom 8:32). Jesus struggles with the pain that this is what his Father is calling him to, the Father he addresses by the most familiar title of *abba*, or "papa," as he begins his prayer of surrender in the garden. Such utter trust recalls the scene of Abraham going up onto the mountain at God's command to offer his only son, Isaac (Gn 22). In a famous rab-binical commentary on Ex 12:42 ("That same night is a vigil to be kept for the Lord by all the Israelites throughout their generations"), the commentator notes that four great events are to happen on Passover night: the creation of the world, the binding of Isaac, the exodus from Egypt, and the coming of the Messiah. Jesus' test of faith is to accept that in surrendering all his hopes and plans to something inconceivable, to which his Father has led him, these four events will find their fulfillment in him. It is little wonder that Matthew has him say, "I am deeply grieved, even to death" (Mt 26:38).

Additional Passages

Gn 22:1–19   Abraham is called to offer up his only son.
Jn 13:1–30   Jesus washes the disciples' feet.

Questions for Reflection

1. Who or what has betrayed me? Have I accepted and forgiven this betrayal?
2. Whom have I abandoned and rejected? Have I sought forgiveness for this failure, and been willing to accept it when offered?
3. Do I allow myself to see only the beauty of nature without looking at its sometimes brutal and uncaring face?

A Final Thought

The activity of God in creation must be precarious. It must proceed by no assured program. Its progress, like every progress of love, must be an angular process—in which every step is a precarious step into the unknown, in which each triumph contains a new potential for tragedy, and each tragedy may be redeemed into a wider triumph.

—William Vanstone

Day 22
Jesus Is Judged—Aloneness and Failure

Prayer Desire

Lord, when my life seems mired in failure, help me to believe that your love always prevails.

Ignatian Focus

Jesus allows his divine status to lie hidden; when he could have unleashed his power and anger upon his enemies he chose to endure the bitter torments that other men and women have experienced in their moments of powerlessness. (*The Spiritual Exercises* 196)

Introduction

We are living in an era that one social commentator has labeled as "the death of the father." From the 1960s onward we have seen a growing rejection of all sorts of authority, especially paternalistic. Partly this has arisen from abhorrence of the sort of tyranny and authoritarianism that marked regimes such as National Socialism in Germany. It also reflects feminist rejection of autocratic and sexist models of governance. Societies that lay great stress on independence, emancipation, and self-fulfillment also have little patience with authority or rank. In such a worldview, surrender of the self is viewed as utterly irreconcilable with genuine autonomy.

The decline of the role of loving authority has been greatly damaging to men. This is not to discount the prejudice and sometimes tyranny that many women have endured from authority figures such as lawyers, doctors, and clerics. Nonetheless, it is critical that men speak out of their own experience, for only then will women know who their true dialogue partners are, for men are their fathers and brothers and lovers. Certainly, in my own country, it has been a commonplace of literature, social analysis, and psychology that the image of "man alone" was a dominant theme in our national consciousness. Fathers who cannot communicate with their sons, lonely and bitter men who recall the fathers who were absent or in hiding behind barricades of silence during their growing years, litter our social and literary landscape. Losing a father's love is devastating for a boy, because it is fathers who provide boys with the energy and courage to go through the processes of separation from their mother, self-identification and differentiation that are critical for growing male identity.

Loss of soul, workaholism, the violence and addiction that mark the lives of many men flow out of this sense of disconnection with their fathers. This makes it impossible for them to enter into intimate relationships or embrace their own mortality. Instead they become consumers, tycoons, or speed and thrill addicts always searching for some attachment that will fill the longing they have for authentic experiences of being, a longing that is often hidden behind walls of anger, shame, or despair.

In Jesus we see a different way of relating as a man. Because he understands his life as one of relationship (Jn 8:28), he has no need to stand on rank but is willing to serve if that best serves the interests of love. Not hooked on power but enlivened by love, he is unafraid to go down into the worst place of human fear, into death itself, convinced that an even greater display of the power of loving relationship will spring out of this abasement. In freely accepting the cross that his Father led him to, Jesus was able to launch a new era of freedom. Tyrants get their own way by their ultimate power of decreeing death. Jesus freely accepted the cross so that his followers would see that death was no longer the ultimate sanction.

Ecological Reflection

Graham Billings's novel *Forbush and the Penguins* traces one summer season of a young biologist taken on as a researcher to monitor the colony of Adélie penguins at Cape Royd in the Antarctic. The colony has been shrinking, and his task is to count the number of breeding pairs and the chicks that survive the season. As he comes to marvel at the patience of the females squatted over their clutch of eggs, he also comes to detest the antics of the skua gulls. Constantly hovering and screeching, they await the moment of inattention as an egg rolls from the small mound of stones that is the penguin's nest, to dive on it, break it open, and scoop out the still warm yolk. He becomes so enraged that one day he declares open war on the gulls. Later, visiting the skua colony, he is appalled to see that the gulls act no differently toward their own. He observes that in any nest in which a second egg is hatched this chick never survives beyond three days. The firstborn uses its greater weight and strength to win most of the food brought by the parents, eventually to drive out the weaker chick, which is then eaten by neighboring adults. As the season ends he looks back and reflects that he has been a total failure. He has lost all sense of scientific objectivity, intervened and disrupted a natural cycle, and is beset by the conviction that he has assisted neither the penguins nor the skuas in any way. In such extremes of cold and ice, life and death are in constant dynamic interaction; nothing that humans can do will make a jot of difference.

As Jesus himself faced an unjust and trumped-up execution, he too must have faced the temptation to abandon all hope simply to accept that sometimes one's best efforts and all one's life energies have been poured out only to meet the stone wall of death.

Scripture Reflection: Lk 23:1–5, 13–23

Then the assembly rose as a body and brought Jesus before Pilate. They began to accuse him saying, "We found this man perverting our nation, forbidding us to pay taxes to the emperor, and saying that he himself is the Messiah, a king." Then Pilate asked him, "Are you the king of the Jews?" He answered, "You say so." Then Pilate said to the chief priests and the crowds, "I find no basis for an accusation against this man." But they were insistent and said, "He stirs up the people by teaching throughout all Judea, from Galilee where he began even to this place."

Pilate then called together the chief priest, the leaders, and the people, and said to them, "You brought me this man as one who was perverting the people; and here I have examined him in your presence and have not found this man guilty of any of your charges against him. Neither has Herod, for he has sent him back to us. Indeed, he has done nothing to deserve death. I will therefore have him flogged and release him."

Then they all shouted out together, "Away with this fellow! Release Barrabas for us!" (This was a man who had been put in prison for an insurrection that had taken place in the city, and for murder.) Pilate, wanting to release Jesus, addressed them again; but they kept shouting, "Crucify, crucify him." A third time he said to them, "Why, what evil has he done? I have found in him no ground for the sentence of death; I will therefore have him flogged and then release him." But they kept urgently demanding with loud shouts that he should be crucified; and their voices prevailed.

Scripture Commentary

Luke's passion story is full of stark irony. The Jewish leaders, despite their hatred of their rulers, are forced to present Jesus' crime as treason to Rome, because they had no power to put to death; they had to present a charge that would worry their rulers. On the other hand, Pilate had no interest in convicting Jesus, but he was subject to political pressure. This leads to bizarre decisions. Pilate declares Jesus innocent and has him flogged. Then he feels compelled to hand him over to death, but makes pointed comments that he is not to blame.

Jesus had to subject himself to this blatant injustice and accept it as one who was powerless. Because of his own inner strength, he could bear this for himself. What must have cost even more was his awareness, despite his own pain and exhaustion, that all that he had loved and given birth to was crumbling all about him. His friends were lost, his mission apparently wiped out. The "little ones," his sheep, the poor and forgotten to whom he had given a new vision of hope, would be scattered and disheartened. All seemed to be lost and terminal, without hope.

Additional Passages

Jn 12:23–33	Unless a grain of wheat falls to the ground and dies.
Mt 26:57–68	Jesus before the Sanhedrin.

Questions for Reflection

1. Have I ever have used my authority or position to prop up the sense of who I am? Why did I do this?

2. Have I ever experienced failure? How did I cope with it and learn from it?

3. Do I carry any "wound of authority," that is, anger or resentment against authority figures for abuses I have suffered in my life?

A Final Thought

Helpless as could be
    Jesus began
the road to Calvary.
Hoots of wild derision
    greeted his
battered, bloody vision.

Alone without a friend
    not a voice
  raised to defend
his head held bowed
  before the
jeering, mocking crowd

The heavy wooden beam
    what a
  torment it did seem
ripping open the gashes
    that were
the legacy of his lashes.

The sight of his mother
    called up
anguish he could not smother.
  Without chance to explain
    each knew
the depth of other's pain.

Jesus tasted deep within
    the dead
  core of all sin,
  that the price to atone
     is to
  suffer utterly alone.

Day 23
King of Love on Calvary

Prayer Desire

I ask God for the grace to let go of my particular hurts, to embrace the universal pain of humankind and of this planet.

Ignatian Focus

I will not entertain any hope of the joy to come until I have walked with Jesus through all the sorrows and sufferings that the world is prey to. (*The Spiritual Exercises* 206)

Introduction

This book is being written against a horizon of impending war: war in the Middle East, acts of terrorism in Asia, and continuing violation of the most basic human rights in part of Africa. Anger and hatred arising out of past injustices have led Arabs and Jews to mutual recrimination. The claim for rights is met by repression; repression gives birth to acts of violence. The West is targeted by Arabs and Muslims for its colonial past and the overwhelming power of its present economic structures. Change seems impossible without loss of power, face, and self-respect. Against this background, John's passion story proclaims something utterly new. Even on the cross Jesus is king, not a king in the sense of a political ruler but one whose love is so powerful it can override death. That very death becomes a unifying act to reunite not just the whole of humanity, but even the whole of creation.

Jesus' crucifixion is the greatest act of love and most potent political symbol for today's world. What Jesus shows us is that someone can be utterly powerless as an individual but radiate a belief in the power of relationship so total and unconditional that nothing, not even death, can obliterate its potency. Theologians use tags like "eternal," "totally free," "loving," and "self-emptying" to describe God. These seem just vacuous labels until we see them made concrete in the response of one lone man on a cross in a gesture of total obedience and surrender. In this act Jesus vicariously takes on all the hatred and hopelessness that victims have known and endured throughout human history.

In striving to unify his own society, Jesus took up the sword of anger. For him, though, this anger was leveled first of all at the injustice and pretence that kept the poor in their place under the pretext of obedience to the law. Anger at some of the Jewish leaders arose not out of personal contempt or jealousy, but because they supported a rigid application of law for their own selfish motives. In his acts Jesus shows the traits of the true nonviolent activist; while urging forgiveness, he will not believe it has truly come until rights and injustices have been addressed. Jesus shows us that anger at evil must be integrated and not ignored for genuine nonviolence to reign. Such nonviolence is the virtue of the strong, not the weak.

The synoptic gospels emphasize the derision and mockery that Jesus suffered. His enemies come to gloat. They take pleasure in the fact that the dying Jesus would have to acknowledge that they had been right all along. It would have been very natural for Jesus to pour out bitter words of anger and denunciation upon them. Instead he prayed for their forgiveness. He excused them for not being able to grasp his love and authenticity or the unique place he held in God's love. Even less could they comprehend the personal love that he held out to them right to the last. It was screened out by self-righteousness, envy, and cynicism—forces of evil. As we will see, John's vision goes even beyond such forgiveness. In the midst of Jesus' passion, John already sees him as having conquered, and the power of this victory is already beginning to transfigure the world, even as the Jewish leaders think that they have won the battle.

Ecological Reflection

The Hebrew scriptures are ambivalent about technology. On one hand, we read the great praise bestowed in Ex 35:30–36:2 on Bezalel, carpenter and metalsmith, and Oholiab, weaver and embroiderer, who constructed the first sanctuary. They are described as being "filled with the Holy Spirit," a phrase normally reserved for kings and prophets. On the other hand, we see Yahweh's deep suspicion of the craftsmen who want to build the great tower at Babel (Gn 11:1–9). What particularly seems to displease Yahweh is the planners' arrogance, their pride at being able to rival God's creativity. Their project ends in dissension and incomprehension, a portent of human tribes' distrust of one another and their mutual rejection. St. Augustine in his commentary on Psalm 95 uses a wonderful image to depict this disintegration of humankind into mutual distrust and incomprehension. He compares it to the dispersion of *Adam* to become *A*natole, *D*ysis, *A*rktos, and *M*esembria, that is, East, West, North, and South. Today, as science and technology create an interconnected planet, it is ironical that postmodern philosophy has gone far in destroying any religious vision that might unify so many different nations and cultures.

This contrasts with the vision of early Christians that Jesus' death was to bring all things into unity. The universal scope of Jesus' redemption is attested to in 2 Cor 5:19, "in Christ God was reconciling the world to himself," while 1 Tm 2:4 and 1 Jn 2:2 insist that God wants all to be saved. Early theologians understood these sayings referred not only to human souls, but to the entire universe. Athanasius, in writing to bishop Adelphius, proclaims that "Christ is . . . the Deliverer of all flesh and of all creation." Jesus' final cry from the cross, "It is finished" (Jn 19:30), does not just mark the end of his physical life; it refers also to the Father's work of creating. Begun in the image of his Son in the original garden, it is fulfilled through the work of his Son in another garden. A world of love and justice will not be complete, however, until some groups that are destroying the environment on which we all depend on for life come to new vision and change the way they consume the world.

Scripture Reflection: Jn 19:13–30

When Pilate heard these words, he brought Jesus outside and sat on the judge's bench at a place called The Stone Pavement, or in Hebrew Gabbatha. Now it was the day of Preparation for the Passover; and it was about noon. He said to the Jews, "Here is your King!" They cried out, "Away with him! Away with him! Crucify him!" Pilate asked them, "Shall I crucify your King?" The chief priests answered, "We have no king but the emperor." Then he handed them over to them to be crucified.

So they took Jesus; and carrying the cross by himself, he went out to what is called The Place of the Skull, which in Hebrew is called

Golgotha. There they crucified him, and with him two others, one on either side, with Jesus between them. Pilate also had an inscription written and put on the cross. It read "Jesus of Nazareth, the King of the Jews." Many of the Jews read this inscription, because the place where Jesus was crucified was near the city; and it was written in Hebrew, in Latin, and in Greek. Then the chief priests of the Jews said to Pilate, "Do not write, 'The King of the Jews,' but, 'This man said, I am King of the Jews.'" Pilate answered, "What I have written I have written." When the soldiers had crucified Jesus, they took his clothes and divided them into four parts, one for each soldier. They also took his tunic; now the tunic was seamless, woven in one piece from the top. So they said to one another, "Let us not tear it, but cast lots for it to see who will get it." This was to fulfill what the scripture says, " They divided my clothes among themselves, and for my clothing they cast lots." And that is what the soldiers did.

Meanwhile, standing near the cross of Jesus were his mother, and his mother's sister, Mary the wife of Clopas, and Mary Magdalene. When Jesus saw his mother and the disciple whom he loved standing beside her, he said to his mother, "Woman, here is your son." Then he said to the disciple, "Here is your mother." And from that hour the disciple took her into his own home.

After this, when Jesus knew that all was now finished, he said (in order to fulfill the scripture), "I am thirsty." A jar full of sour wine was standing there. So they put a sponge full of the wine on a branch of hyssop and held it to his mouth. When Jesus had received the wine, he said, "It is finished." Then he bowed his head and gave up his spirit.

Scripture Commentary

In the development of the four gospels, the account of the Lord's Supper is one of the earliest elements. Part of the reason for this is that these accounts were the core of the liturgy when the first Christians met to celebrate Jesus' rising on the first day of the week. So they and the passion story that they introduce were never separated from the passage to glory that Jesus achieved in his resurrection. This link between death and exultation shines out most clearly in John's account of Jesus' suffering and death. For John, the passion is Jesus' definitive revelation as king, whereas the theme of the kingdom or realm of God, so important in the other gospels, hardly occurs in John at all.

John marks this theme of kingship in three related themes: Jesus' return to the Father (Jn 13:1), the beginning of his exultation or being raised up (Jn 8:28, 12:32), and his induction into the glory of God (Jn 13:31–32, 17:1). The first dialogue with Pilate introduces the nature of Jesus' kingship (Jn 18:37), but it is the second part of this trial that discloses the true basis of his title, namely, that he is the Son of God (Jn 19:7). This passage on which we now meditate spells out how John sees that kingship exhibited even in Jesus' very act of dying. First, Jesus alone, not any helper, carries his cross to Calvary; in this he fulfills the Old Testament typology of Isaac carrying the wood for his own sacrifice (Gn 22:1–14). The sign hanging above him to which the Jewish leaders vehemently objected stresses in a public and universal way that he is king in Greek, Latin, and Hebrew so that all may read. In his last moments John has no mocking crowd to berate Jesus; this is a private and privileged moment shared only with the beloved disciple, his mother, and a couple of the other women closest to him. He is in control of the process until the end, when he finally gives up his Spirit to fulfill the command given by the Father to drink fully from the cup he was given (Jn 18:11).

Additional Passages

Phil 3:1–16	I can give up all things for the sake of having Christ.
Rom 8:18–39	Jesus takes up all the groaning of creation.

Questions for Reflection

1. What are the targets of my anger? Do I use my anger constructively to bring about positive change?
2. Can I identify any areas of my life where I need to enthrone Jesus as "king of love" to respond to otherwise hopeless situations?
3. What social or ecological initiatives could I become part of in my district that would step outside the political, social, or religious groups in which I normally operate?

A Final Thought

This tree [Jesus' cross], wide as the heavens itself, has grown up into heaven from the earth. It is an immortal growth and towers twixt heaven and earth. It is the fulcrum of all things and the place where they are all at rest. It is the foundation of the round world, the center of the cosmos. In it all the diversities in our human nature are formed into a unity. It is held together by invisible nails of the spirit so that it may not break loose from the divine. It touches the highest summits of heaven and makes the earth firm beneath its foot, and it grasps the middle region between them with immeasurable arms.

—St. Hippolytus of Rome

Day 24
Wilderness Day

Prayer Desire

I ask Jesus to be with me in whatever wilderness he wants to share with me.

Scripture Reflection

Mk 14:1–15:41   Jesus' passion and death.

Day 25
Death and Repose

Prayer Desire

I ask God to help me to learn to grieve with Mary, sorrowing over what is lost, hoping for what is still to be revealed.

Ignatian Focus

Throughout this day I ponder on the mystery of the sundering of Jesus' body and spirit, how he was laid to rest, and Mary's sorrow, exhaustion, and loneliness as she faced this long day. (*The Spiritual Exercises* 208)

Introduction

About six years ago a couple who were friends of mine were parted when the wife died of cancer. The last time I went to visit them, Mary was lying in a large double bed. All medical treatment was finished, save for a morphine pump to control her pain. The visit was particularly poignant because both of us knew that it would be the last time we would speak together. Despite the sorrow, we were surrounded by joyous mementos of life. Covering her bed was a huge quilt into which had been worked scenes taken from photos of family festivals: baptisms, wedding anniversaries, Christmas gatherings, holidays at the beach. As she waited to die, the rich tapestry of her life gave witness to all she been and done for others.

Modern techniques by which small electrodes can be used to stimulate given areas of the brain have confirmed the close connection between memory and emotion. The triggering of long-dormant memories by such stimulation can evoke deep and powerful emotions linked to a particular person or place. Many of us will have experienced the natural counterpart to this; a hint of a perfume or a profile glimpsed from a moving vehicle will summon up a vivid recollection and powerful feelings of someone we have not seen or thought of for many years. In a certain way the past never dies; it is only covered over with deep layers of sedimentation.

It is against this background that we can understand the ancient Christian idea of "the harrowing of hell." The extract from the Easter homily of an ancient Christian author read at the Office of Readings for Easter Saturday captures it so well. It pictures Jesus bearing his burial shroud visiting the dark caverns of the underworld to call forth Adam and all the faithful men and women who have waited long for his coming, to bring them out into light and life once more.

Ecological Reflection

Advances in medical technology have prompted two current social trends. The first is the growing use of cryopreservation, freezing techniques to keep tissues from dead bodies in a state of preservation for long periods. First used for mummifying beloved pets, it is now being used to keep human brains and even entire bodies in the hope that some time in the future medical technology will reach the point that such bodies can be reanimated. The second trend is the extension of medical gerontology to keep elderly people in good health and ward off the very advent of aging. Some doctors are talking about keeping people fit and active until they are 130 or 140 years old.

The ecological consequences of such proposals are vast. This is highlighted by current population trends. In many parts of the developing world, such as Mexico or the Philippines, one of the greatest social and economic pressures is the shortage of resources to meet the needs of the youthful population of workers and students. In other parts of the planet such as Europe birthrates have fallen below replacement levels. This means not only that there are fewer and fewer productive workers to support many elderly, but that in relative terms many citizens of such areas will be using a huge amount of resources compared to the citizens of lesser-developed regions.

It not does seem a coincidence to me that this urgent need to prolong life as much as possible is becoming a trend at the same time that belief in any sort of life after death is declining in nations that were once predominantly Christian. Not a few postmodern Christians now regard belief in life after death as a hangover from ages in which hope for immortality was the only solace in lives of short and squalid brutality. They believe that modern science and philosophy have discredited such "myths." To my understanding, they have discounted something that is quite central to a Christian vision of the cosmos, that there are personal bonds and influence that reach across and beyond death. This truth is central to the experience of Mary and the first disciples in the events that followed Christ's death.

Scripture Reflection: Jn 19:38–41

After these things, Joseph of Arimathea, who was a disciple of Jesus, though a secret one because of his fear of the Jews, asked Pilate to let him take away the body of Jesus. Pilate gave him permission; so he came and removed his body. Nicodemus, who had first come to Jesus by night, also came, bringing a mixture of myrrh and aloes, weighing about a hundred pounds. They took the body of Jesus and wrapped it with the spices in linen cloths, according to the burial custom of the Jews. Now there was a garden in the place where he was crucified, and in the garden there was a new tomb in which no one had ever been laid. And so, because it was the Jewish day of Preparation, and the tomb was nearby, they laid Jesus there.

Scripture Commentary

This passage, brief as it is, makes several important points. Several men whose position made it impolitic to be associated with Jesus while he was alive, immediately after his death find the courage to profess their allegiance to him. His mode of burial is utterly different from the usual victims of Roman executions, interment in a shallow common grave where they could be scavenged by wandering animals. He is anointed with a huge weight of spices, what might be used for a royal burial, and swathed in linen bands (different than Mark's use of a burial shroud). The body is buried according to Jewish custom, that is, it is not cut or opened in any way (for it is to rise again). The new tomb in the new garden clearly carries connotations of a heavenly paradise such as the one that Jesus promised the criminal crucified along with him (see Lk 23:43). More pragmatically, it accentuates the uniqueness of where he lay; there could be no confusion as to where he was or which body was his when Mary Magdalene came seeking him on the Sunday morning.

Additional Passages

Is 52:13–53:12   The fourth song of the Suffering Servant.
2 Cor 5:16–21   God made the sinless one into sin on account of us.

Questions for Reflection

1. What has my experience of grief been? Full, painful, or still blocked? Why?
2. Am I able to talk with Jesus about my own death and face my fears and uncertainties together with him?

3. Do I visit wilderness, farms, or woodlands to see there some of the natural processes of birth and death that surround us, even as we ignore them?

A Final Thought

Healthy children will not fear life if their elders have integrity enough not to fear death.

—Erik Erikson

Week 4 *Four*

RISING TO NEW LIFE

Many of the veterans who came back from the Vietnam War in the sixties and seventies, when they finally could talk about it, told of the desensitization that grew like a citadel within them to protect them from the memories of ruined villages, of children shattered by mines and helicopter-launched rockets, of brutal massacres of old men and women by either side. It was a desensitization so deep-seated and effective that it locked them behind walls of silence even in their marriages and most intimate relations. Retreatants' grief and hurts are seldom of that order. Nonetheless, on television and in newspapers we constantly come across scenes of violence and hatred—in Iraq, Zimbabwe, or wherever today's battle zone is. When these become uncomfortable or too pressing, we can close our eyes or turn to the next page. Having stood beside Jesus as he embraced betrayal and death for all people, that option is not so automatic or available as it once was. For those who have entered deeply into the process of the third week, identification with the sufferings of the innocent remains an enduring part of their lives

Christ gives his disciples a lively awareness that his paschal journey is not yet completed. He continues to identify with and be present to the pains of innocent men and women, offering their Calvaries to the Father. Jesus also makes retreatants acutely aware during this week that his very physical identification with all the hungry and oppressed

(Mt 25:31–46) must be their vision too. As the retreat fades in intensity, so this acute sense of God's continuing suffering in this world may grow dim, but there is always a persistent residue of awareness that all the agony of the world is held in God and that we too are called at times to let those wounds be ours.

The second fruit of this week is the opening of retreatants' eyes to the different ways that men and women struggle to cope with their sufferings. Far from creating feelings of superiority, this can help retreatants to see more objectively and compassionately. They understand why some adopt fearful and obsessive religions while others rest their faith in the sureness of science and technological progress. In the last fifty years many men and women have turned to the spate of books and psychological movements that have exalted the power of positive thought, movements insisting that people should be always be happy and positive. Any hint of depression, guilt, or remorse is a weakness to be avoided. In the spiritual void of today other people have turned to New Age philosophies or to Eastern religions such as Buddhism or Sufi mysticism.

Thoreau's observation that most men (and women) lead lives of quiet desperation has become a bit trite by now, but still contains much truth. Graduates of the third week do not congratulate themselves on becoming aware of the desperation hidden behind the masks of many of their companions and fellow workers. Rather, they discover a deep well of compassion to which they must return again and again. Often they will find that the scope of their compassion has widened. They become alert to the cycles of life and death in the trees and hedgerows around them and in the multitude of creatures that make their homes there. Many become more sensitive to the struggles of the planet, concerned about poisoned lakes and seas, the threat to the survival of the last remnants of the once great schools of cod and turbot in the Grand Banks off Newfoundland. Their journey to the wellsprings of human frailty and aloneness has touched our human rootedness in and dependence on nature, so that vision flows out from those roots to the land, water, and food chains upon which we humans draw for survival.

Another fruit of this week is a conviction of the need for reconciliation. Directors often use the slogan "Awareness heals" when their directees are enduring painful discoveries about their own self-deception or the hidden dynamics of a family life they once uncritically lionized. Sadly, the slogan is only half true. Awareness is the beginning of healing, but it is not enough in itself. Often resentments or enmity harbored for siblings, parents, or former colleagues have to be aired. Sometimes this must be done face-to-face. Where that is not possible or profitable, there may be the need for a period of journaling, counseling, or some honest letters. Verbalizing fears and resentments both makes their power tangible and allows it to be defused. Likewise, the response of a former colleague or family member can open up whole new vistas of self-discovery or intimations into the working of communities that were a closed door up to that moment. This in turn leads to much new work. The need for personal acceptance of hurts incurred and wounds inflicted on others may become clearer as retreatants return to environments that seemed to be fixed and comfortable but are now seen with new eyes. Having walked with Jesus during his arrest, interrogations, tortures, humiliation, the trudge to Golgotha, and his long-drawn-out execution, those who make the Ignatian retreat know that conversion does not come all at once. There will be moments of intense insight, but also times of struggle to distance oneself from old habits and patterns of interpretation developed over years.

Seeing Jesus' acceptance of humiliation can also help retreatants, as nothing else can do, to believe in the humility of God. Knowing that their God is so weak and approachable lets them come out from behind their masks of deference and pretense to speak to God as one does to a friend—even to expressing the anger and frustration in their lives and their resentment of the God who put them there.

The final fruit of this week is a growing sense of integration into the life of the Trinity. From the first meditation of Week One, Ignatius encourages the retreatant to finish off each time of prayer with a colloquy with Christ. This is a time of familiar and simple converse in which the one who is concluding the time of prayer chats and reflects together with Christ on what he or she has seen, heard, and noticed. From the middle of the first week Ignatius introduces the Triple Colloquy. Not only do retreatants converse with Jesus in this way, they also talk with the Father and with Mary, the mother of Christ, asking them to help provide greater insight into the meaning of events in which they were often intimate players. This habit of frequent discourse and mutual sharing gradually builds up a sense that the inner dynamic of Jesus' ministry and of the retreat is that of a shared journey. The structure of the retreatants' relations with God becomes less and less unitarian and more and more trinitarian.

The great transition that marks the passage into the final week of the Exercises is the discovery of joy. This may come at different stages and depth, depending on personality, but it is the marker of how genuine each retreatant's identification with Jesus has been. Since the reality of the resurrection is not open to human reason or imagination, it can only be discovered by encountering the risen Lord. So the more deeply one has given one's heart, support, and hope to the lone and suffering Christ, the more intense will be the joy and overwhelming delight in meeting him risen and triumphant. As Elie Wiesel, survivor of Nazi death camps expressed it, "No one is as capable of gratitude as one who has emerged from the kingdom of night."

This joy is likewise a fruit of love. Having seen how Christ's trust and surrender to his Father have brought him to such triumph, many retreatants will also want to let go of their remaining fears and surrender themselves totally to God. They experience this in no way as slavery but as a great act of liberation, for it is mutual. They have a deep certainty that whatever they give to God is being returned to them a hundredfold. Jesus now comes to the retreatant as one who consoles, who wants to repair the community by renewing trust and assuring forgiveness. His assurance is that he will always be there to reinvigorate and give new hope, despite the retreatant's weakness. He continues to live on, bearing the wounds of human weakness in the scars he carries, but now without flaw or limitation.

The paradox of the wounded healer is also a deep part of the scriptural passages that describe the postresurrection events. For while a retreatant may sense the power of the gifts of the Holy Spirit blossoming within her (Gal 5:22), she may also experience the whole gamut of negative feelings echoed in the scriptural passages that describe the postresurrection events. She may discover that joy, fear, and doubt can walk hand in hand. Like the women at the tomb, she too may be terrified (Lk 24:5), she may be doubtful if it is possible to believe such an extraordinary story (Mk 16:11), yet still have a heart jumping with joy (Lk 24:41).

This sense of joy often intensifies as retreatants work through Ignatius's Contemplation to Attain the Love of God. This title is something of a misnomer as the aim of the reflection is not so much to gain love (by this stage such love abounds) but more to see the way in which God loves, and to be encouraged to love God, all other people, and the whole of creation in this way. It is like nothing else in the entire retreat. Consisting of four brief points, it is often spread over successive days: the first point on day one, the next on day two, the third and fourth on the final day, with usually a repetition of the exercise as a whole with which to conclude.

In his brief introduction Ignatius stresses that love is based on acts, not words, and is a sharing in each other's goods. In the first point he asks the retreatant to recall all the blessings of creation and redemption and how God has bestowed all of these, but most of all the gift of himself. The second point turns toward the world and invites the retreatants to give thanks for plants and animals, and all the diversity, richness, and sensations of nature, then to see themselves as images of God within that creation. In the third point he focuses on the work and value of all these creatures and how God conserves, cares, and nourishes them all, making them available for human use. The final point sees all blessings and gifts, all virtues and life as coming from God, like warmth pouring out of the sun or water from a fountain (*The Spiritual Exercises* 230–37). The dynamic here is as if the work of transformation draws retreatants to their innermost depths, to find there a new entranceway to creation, so that seeing it with new eyes, they will love and work within it in a completely new way. The contemplation serves as a way back into the ordinary world after the intense experiences of the retreat. It is a specific example of Ignatius's own motto "To find God in all things."

Day 26
Jesus Is Risen

Prayer Desire

I ask that I may know a deep and growing joy in Jesus risen to new life.

Ignatian Focus

I consider how Jesus' divine character, which seemed to be hidden during his passion, now shows itself in his resurrection to powerful effect. (*The Spiritual Exercises* 223)

Introduction

Though some ecologists do not want to distinguish between different species, when it comes to the value of life it seems clear that the more complex the nervous system and social life of a creature are, the more it reflects individuality and uniqueness. Living in a country where there are about ten times more sheep than there are humans, I do not find it hard to state that sheep personalities do not strike one as radically different from one another. Even on farms where lambs are given to children as pets, the disappearance of a loved pet in favor of a newborn cuddly lamb does not generally seem to give rise to great loss and grief.

In contrast, one of the noticeable characteristics of the resurrection stories in the gospels is how different they are, and how these differences reflect the diverse personalities to whom Jesus shows himself. We see this in the way John's account (Jn 20:11–18) reflects the deep personal attachment of Mary Magdalene to her friend, as compared to the ambiguity of the two disciples returning to Emmaus (Lk 24:13–35) who encounter the risen Lord after a very different sort of dialogue. In the meditations that Ignatius proposes for Week Four of the Exercises, he is scrupulous in following the structure of the gospel accounts, except when it comes to a risen appearance of Jesus to his mother, Mary that he proposes as the first meditation of the fourth week.

In this instance Ignatius is not just following ancient Catholic tradition, but also reflects the unique role that Mary takes on as the final days of her son's life draw near. At the annunciation and when the shepherds acclaim Jesus' birth at Bethlehem, Mary is singled out as a hearer of the word (Lk 2:19–20). Her role as mother is marked out as going far beyond normal Jewish expectations of family relations, for example, when she is the voice called to underline Jesus' prior loyalty to his Father when he is lost in the Temple (Lk 2:49) and again when she has to acknowledge the new basis of Jesus' family of faith (Mk 3:34–35). She must have endured public ridicule and shame at

Nazareth, where Jesus was rejected but she had to stay on. This prepared her to slip gradually into the role of disciple, which would end with her final total act of surrender to God at the foot of the cross. Many who have shared Mary's grief as part of their retreat have sensed that her sorrow was unique, very different from the inconsolable loss felt by Lazarus or Mary Magdalene, or the shame and anguish that gripped Peter. Still open to God, Mary may well have intuited that there was something immense yet to come, that Jesus' journey was not yet finished, and that another visitation and return to the hills of Galilee still awaited her.

Ecological Reflection

In 1961 the first SETI (Search for Extraterrestrial Intelligence) conference occurred in the United States. One of the outcomes of this first conference was the promulgation of the Drake equation, named after Dr. Frank Drake. Taking into account factors such as atmosphere, size, temperature, density, and many other variables, it attempted to estimate the number of possible planets in our universe that might host intelligent life. Depending on how stringently scientists interpreted each criterion, candidates were estimated as anywhere between a thousand to a million. The assumption behind such debate since then has been that planet earth is nothing special; the life we see here is just one instance of a phenomenon that is bound to be repeated all over our universe. Detecting that life has been viewed as the main challenge.

Over the last decade there has been a marked shift in this viewpoint. A good example comes in Peter Ward and Donald Brownlee's 2000 work, *Rare Earth: Why Complex Life Is Uncommon in the Universe.* They are part of a group of scientists who, while not discounting the possibility of life elsewhere in the universe, have underlined the many extraordinary physical and chemical factors that must coexist, at astoundingly high odds, for life to emerge. Another instance is Michael Denton's 1998 book, *Nature's Destiny,* in which he examines the highly distinctive properties of water, iron, energy from our sun, and many other factors to show how unique and highly tuned they are to the emergence and maintenance of human life. These writers come from a scientific rather than religious perspective. Nonetheless, the sense of wonder that we see in their texts is not too far from the sense of joy and awe that we find in the biblical resurrection texts as the first Christians have their eyes opened to what can only be described as a re-creation of their universe.

Scripture Reflection: Jn 20:11–18

But Mary stood weeping outside the tomb. As she wept, she bent over to look into the tomb; and she saw two angels in white, sitting where the body of Jesus had been lying, one at the head and the other at the feet. They said to her, "Woman, why are you weeping?" She said to them, "They have taken away my Lord, and I do not know where they have laid him." When she had said this, she turned around and saw Jesus standing there, but she did not know that it was Jesus. Jesus said to her, "Woman, why are you weeping? Whom are you looking for?" Supposing him to be the gardener, she said to him, "Sir, if you have carried him away, tell me where you have laid him, and I will take him away." Jesus said to her, "Mary!" She turned and said to him in Hebrew "Rabbouni!" (which means Teacher). Jesus said to her, "Do not hold on to me, because I have not yet ascended to the Father. But go to my brothers and say to them, 'I am ascending to my Father and your Father, to my God and your God.'" Mary Magdalene went and announced to the disciples, "I have seen the Lord"; and she told them that he had said these things to her.

Scripture Commentary

It is clear that the risen Jesus looks very different from the man we met in the Weeks Two and Three of the Exercises. Even those closest to him, such as Mary and Peter, do not recognize him at first. He also has a disconcerting way of arriving without warning and disappearing just as suddenly. In establishing his identity, it is usually some familiar word or gesture that opens the disciples' eyes. In the first creation account Adam established his relationship with the animals by naming them, seeing their particular place and niche in creation; with Eve he recognized and announced to all who could hear what God had shaped, woman, the bringer of life. In proclaiming her name, Mary, the new Adam in the new garden prophesies and creates a new role and identity for this born-again woman. But all cannot be as it was before, for Jesus too has been reborn out of death; Mary cannot cling to the same relationship as before. She still has his love, but her response must now shift to going out and proclaiming to those who have not yet heard the astounding news. She becomes the disciple to the disciples.

This account underlines another factor common to many of the appearance narratives, the great importance of witness. The experience of the risen Jesus by one of his followers opens the way for his revelation to another. Yet it is clear that in this paradoxical world, seeing is not necessarily believing. Nor is hearing about somebody else's seeing enough—as we will find with the two travelers walking to Emmaus.

Additional Passages

Mk 16:1–8   Jesus appears to the women at the sepulcher.
Eph 1:3–14   The mystery of God's plans revealed in Christ.

Questions for Reflection

1. Do I deeply accept my own uniqueness and irreplaceability as a person? Does it bring me joy?
2. What steps could I take to learn about the remarkable character of life, especially human life, on this planet?
3. Have I ever asked Jesus to come to me in surprising and unexpected ways in my daily routine? If not, why?

A Final Thought

As dawn cast a livid scar across the sky
Mary hurried to the tomb through streets heavy with morning.
The feet that once she'd dried would no longer bring good news
but now she would bind his wounds with loving care.
Racing back to tell Peter and John that the stone was gone
one thought held all: where had they hidden her love?
Tell me, gardener, where is my love?
Is hardly a sane question at six at a rock tomb.
His response, Mary, was an echo of past days

and an identity rediscovered at his feet,
but also a gentle summons to bury the dead.
The Jesus who calls me today is not
the glorious remembered of yesterday, but a man
died and reborn over and over. That ageless
moment of recognition "I have seen the Lord"
now becomes a sign of witness and a call to all.

Day 27
Seeing With New Eyes

Prayer Desire

I pray for the grace to recognize the risen Jesus in the hidden ways he comes to me.

Ignatian Focus

I reflect how Jesus consoles his followers, in the way that friends go about consoling one another in times of distress. (*The Spiritual Exercises* 224)

Introduction

One of the scenarios for the death of our universe is heat death, the gradual dissipation of all heat and energy. As all bodies' temperatures drop closer and closer to absolute zero, life and light slowly fade to leave dark and lifeless skeletons moving endlessly out into the depths of space. Some commentators have foreseen ways in which, they believe, human life can persist for a very long time even within this picture. They know that many human organs can presently be replaced by artificial substitutes, and are aware of research into the way in which human brains could be linked to and subsumed within highly complex computers. Such computers could be networked over vast distances to retain intelligent awareness even at the lowest levels of energy use. This scenario is a replay of very ancient Gnostic picture of human existence, disembodied spirits finally freed from the burden of weak and inferior bodies.

I see a parallel behind such projections of the human future and a tendency to explain away the Christian story of the resurrection through psychological and sociological models. The German theologian Rudolf Bultmann's project of trying to demythologize the gospels, removing from them anything of the supernatural or miraculous that did not fit with modern scientific and critical thought, still exerts its sway. Perhaps a purely inner sense of Christ's triumph over death might have moved the disciples to go out and proclaim his teaching. What they would have been presenting, however, would be more a glorious memory than a living presence. It would have lacked bite: for resurrection to have depth and substance, it must be bodily. Human lives are lives lived in the soil, among the beasts, not in the mind. Yeats show a fine appreciation of this in his poem "A Prayer for Old Age," saying in one stanza:

> God guard me from the thoughts men think
> In the mind alone;
> He that sings a lasting song
> Thinks in a marrow bone.

Tradition has captured this intuition in its insistence that at the resurrection it was not a soul, memory, or spirit that was raised but a body. We know little of the properties of that body. I imagine it to be like the condition of the universe in "Planck's time," the tiny fraction of a second that the primordial mass of the universe existed before it began to expand in the big bang. What we do know is that there is continuity between Jesus' earthly body and the person that his friends rediscovered. Such continuity is critical. It assures us that Christ is part of the brutal things that humans do to one another and to nature; he could die. But, on the other hand, Jesus could not be confined by the limits of our physical universe, even death. Within thirty years of Jesus' death Paul was already linking Christ's death to the renewal of the cosmos through the event of the resurrection.

Ecological Reflection

Part of the Stoic and alchemical traditions of the Middle Ages was to depict the earth as a geocosm, that is, as a body, particularly the female body. Like that body, it was a living organic unit. Mineral deposits were the veins of the body, natural springs its blood system. Female reproductive and nursing powers were like the earth's capacity to give birth to stones and metals within its womb. Though such a vision could lead to gross exploitation of both women and the earth, it did capture the sense that the human body is a microcosm (a world in miniature), while the planet (or the whole universe) is the macrocosm that it mirrors. Body and planet are similar too in that each is really a communion of different entities. Bodies are made up of a vast diversity of cells, each of which contains many semi-independent organelles. So too the planet is a constantly interacting and self-regulating balance of hydrosphere, lithosphere, and atmosphere. Just as humans suffer from imbalances of too much fat or too many invasive microbes, so too does the planet sicken from too much waste or nondegradable toxins such as PCBs or dioxins.

This mirror imaging of body and planet is just one of the ways in which some of the mathematical patterns found in the human brain are echoed in the structures of the physical world. Einstein's famous conclusion from special relativity of the relationship between matter and energy came nearly forty years before its implications were demonstrated in the explosion of the first atomic bomb. Centuries ago, the Italian mathematician Leonardo Fibonacci discovered the amazing properties of the sequence named after him (0, 1, 1, 2, 3, 5, 8, 13, 21, etc; the sum of the two previous numbers making the next number). This pattern was found to be the basis of the harmonies in certain types of music and in some styles of architecture such as Gothic cathedrals. It can also predict the number of petals contained in the concentric rings of complex flower heads. Even without any explicit mathematical knowledge, the right brain seems to be able to recognize this pattern and draw pleasure from it, describing its effects in words like "symmetry," "rhythm," and "harmony." The most widely used is "beauty." Beauty is something embedded in the innermost patterns of nature. This led Poincaré, the nineteenth-century Frenchman who was probably the last universal genius in mathematics, to declare, "The most useful combinations are precisely the most beautiful." Not surprisingly, then, humans often encounter God in the most bodily moments like eating and drinking, something discovered by two disciples as they returned to the village of Emmaus after Jesus' death.

Scripture Reflection: Lk 24:13–35

Two of them were going to a village called Emmaus . . . talking with each other about all these things that had happened. While they were talking and discussing, Jesus himself came near and went with them, but their eyes were kept from recognizing him. And he said to them, "What are you discovering with each other while you walk along? . . . Cleopas answered him, "Are you the only stranger in Jerusalem who does not know the things that have taken place there in these days?" He asked them, "What things?" They replied, "The things about Jesus of Nazareth, who was a prophet mighty in deed before God and before all the people, and how our chief priests and leaders handed him over to be condemned to death and crucified him. But we had hoped that he was the one to redeem Israel. . . . Moreover, some women of our group astounded us. They were at the tomb early this morning, and when they did not find his body there, they came back and told us that they had indeed seen a vision of angels who said that he was alive. Some of those who were with us went to the tomb and found it just as the women had said; but they did not see him." Then he said to them, "Oh, how foolish you are, and how slow of heart to believe all that the prophets have declared! Was it not necessary that the Messiah should suffer these things and then enter into his glory?" Then beginning with Moses and all the prophets, he interpreted to them the things about himself in all the scriptures.

As they came near the village to which they were going, he walked ahead as if he were going on. But they urged him strongly, saying, "Stay with us, because it is almost evening and the day is now nearly over." So he went in to stay with them. When he was at table with them, he took bread, blessed and broke it, and gave it to them. Then their eyes were opened, and they recognized him; and he vanished from their sight. They said to each other, "Were not our hearts burning within us while he was talking to us on the road, while he was opening the scriptures to us?" That same hour they got up and returned to Jerusalem; and they found the eleven and their companions gathered together. They were saying, "The Lord has risen indeed, and he has appeared to Simon!" Then they told what had happened on the road, and how he had been made known to them in the breaking of the bread.

Scripture Commentary

The first point that strikes us about this passage is that the two disciples are quickly heading away from Jerusalem, the place for Luke that is the goal of Jesus' long journey. Their haste reflects not just a sense of failure but has overtones of desertion, shame, and guilt. From their own admission not only was their expectation of Jesus (a prophet to free the people) frankly political, but they also would lend no credence to the women's story of a risen Jesus. It is only when they begin to entertain this stranger whose insight has begun to grip them that their vision begins to change.

Critically, it is at the breaking of the bread that their eyes are opened. The ritual words, "took, blessed, broke" are the same words as those used to describe Jesus' actions at the Last Supper (Lk 22:19) and at the multiplication of the loaves (Lk 9:16). Even more, it is likely that some distinctive way of breaking the bread was part of the pattern familiar to the Lucan church in their celebration of the Lord's Supper. What happens next is critical: "Then their eyes were opened" (Lk 24:31). The eminent scripture scholar Tom Wright believes that the couple is very likely to be the husband and wife Cleopas and Mary (cf. Jn 19:35). This would strengthen the connection to the story of Adam and Eve in chapter 3 of Genesis. It is only after they have betrayed God and each other by eating the apple that "their eyes were opened" (Gn 3:7). The Greek used by Luke is almost identical to the Greek translation of the Genesis text. Wright also mentions that this meal is the eighth described in Luke's gospel, the seventh being the Last Supper. We understand that as a way of indicating that the week of the first creation is ended, now God's new world has begun. Likewise the exile, not just of Israel but of the whole human family, is over. Certainly the result is very clear for the couple. Their sadness and slowness is transformed into joy and exultation, and despite the lateness of the hour they head instantly back to Jerusalem to take up the task of being the bringers of the good news of the gospel, "Christ is risen."

Additional Passages

Mt 28:1–10   Jesus appears to the women.
1 Cor 15:20–28   Christ is the first fruits of all that will be raised.

Questions for Reflection

1. How can I best revere my body as something that will be raised in the image of Christ?
2. Are there ways I can offer hospitality to bodies that presently seem aged, disfigured, or ugly?
3. Is my experience of parish or Sunday eucharist very privatized and lacking in symbolic richness? Could I help the community to recreate something of the discovery of the disciples on the road to Emmaus?

A Final Thought

To be of the earth is to know
    the restlessness of being a seed
    the darkness of being planted
    the struggle toward the light
    the pain of growth into the light
    the joy of bursting and bearing fruit
    the love of being food for someone
    the scattering of your seeds
    the decay of the seasons
    the mystery of death
    and the miracle of birth.

—John Soos

Day 28
Laying Old Ghosts to Rest

Prayer Desire

I pray for the grace to let go completely of the shame of the past, to embrace the joy that my risen Lord offers me.

Ignatian Focus

Love consists in mutual sharing. The lover gives and shares with the beloved what he has, and the beloved in turn gives what she has. (*The Spiritual Exercises* 231)

Introduction

The doctrine of original sin has been disturbing for many people. It was often presented as guilt that all of us carry, a burden of shame that taints even the most innocent. This seemed an unjust imposition, a way of devaluing people that undermined the goodness of life and the joy of creation. So it is not too surprising that many people came to ignore or downplay the doctrine. New understanding is shedding a lot of light on the meaning of this teaching. A truer way of seeing it is not as guilt but as entrapment, a universal victimhood that ensnares all of us. It is something akin to the situation of the victims of child abuse; they find themselves enmeshed in misery and degradation that they had no part in causing, yet whose effects they seem doomed to carry.

Such victimhood has strong links with the practice of scapegoating. Groups use scapegoating as a way to create unity by excluding and victimizing someone who is smaller, weaker, or different. The group's failings are blamed on this outsider, who is then targeted and excluded, thus helping to unite the group in mutual solidarity and bloodguilt. The resentment and anger occasioned by such behavior provokes payback and revenge; a cycle of violence and counterviolence comes to birth, such as we see in Palestine and Israel.

By itself such a cycle is self-perpetuating and impossible to break. The good news that Christ brings us is that this state of sin can be broken through reconciliation. Christian reconciliation is both forgiveness and the refusal to keep on blaming. This is extraordinarily difficult in human terms, one of the hardest of human choices. We cannot do it alone, only with the power of the Holy Spirit.

Many retreatants are puzzled that Ignatius seems virtually to ignore the role of the Holy Spirit in the life of the Christian. There are some good historical reasons for this. The theology of the Spirit was weak in the Western church in the sixteenth and seventeenth centuries. Those few who had stressed it, such as the Anabaptists, were mainly remembered for the heresy and social upheaval associated with their followers. Such suspicion was the last thing Ignatius wanted. As it was, he ran foul of the Inquisition about a dozen times, especially because they could not understand how an unlettered layman (as he was in his early years) was able to teach spiritual principles with such authority.

In effect, however, the Exercises are steeped in a sense of the movement and freedom of the Spirit. We see this in Ignatius's trust of the power of active imagination when he encourages the retreatant to enter the scriptures with no preconceived outcome. Instead he trusts in the freedom of the dialogue between retreatants and their directors. The importance of the Holy Spirit is also clear in the importance Ignatius places on the Rules for the Discernment of Spirits in the first two weeks of the retreat. It is evident too in his advice to retreatants continually to ask Christ to shape their hearts and to move their feelings in accordance with the mystery being entered into. When it comes to the time after the retreat, Ignatius has very little in the way of explicit directions, simply encouraging the practice of daily prayer, examination of conscience, and use of the Rules for the Discernment of Spirits. In this he follows the practice of St. Paul when he trusts his converts to the guidance of the Spirit; there cannot be a detailed program for spiritual life, for this is shaped by the Spirit in accordance with the gifts and needs of each Christian (see Gal 5:16–23). It is particularly in the postresurrection meditations that we see this freedom blossoming, especially when it comes to liberation from all the shackles and burdens of the past.

Ecological Reflection

One of the main symbols for the Holy Spirit in the scriptures is that of breath or wind. Wind can be the tornado that rips apart houses and farmsteads destroying thirty years of work in thirty seconds. Yet it is also the planet's breath of life. Without wind there would be no circulation of air. The poles would be a zone of relentless ice and snow; the equatorial belts would be a torrid and unrelieved furnace, hostile to all life. Wind brings the rains of the longed-for monsoon, providing growth and sweetness to the parched fields. It carries the seeds that bring new life to continents, as well as the moisture and the soil in which they can grow. Wind is the joy of a breeze on a summer's day, the zest that drives windsurfers gliding across the curling waves; it is the chinook that breaks the crushing grip of ice and snow after the hardest of winters. Without wind there would be no life. Without the Spirit there would be no forgiveness, no hope of life re-created.

Scripture Reflection: Jn 20:19–29

When it was evening on that day, the first day of the week, and the doors of the house where the disciples had met were locked for fear of the Jews, Jesus came and stood among them and said, "Peace be with you." After he said this, he showed them his hands and his side. Then the disciples rejoiced when they saw the Lord. Jesus said to them again, "Peace be with you. As the Father has sent me, so I send you." When he had said this, he breathed on them and said, "Receive the Holy Spirit. If you forgive the sins of any, they are forgiven them; if you retain the sins of any, they are retained."

But Thomas (who was called the Twin), one of the twelve, was not with them when Jesus came. So the other disciples told him, "We have seen the Lord." But he said to them, "Unless I see the mark of the nails in his hands, and put my finger in the mark of the nails and my hand in his side, I will not believe."

A week later his disciples were again in the house, and Thomas was with them. Although the doors were shut, Jesus came and stood among them and said, "Peace be with you." Then he said to Thomas, "Put your finger here and see my hands. Reach out your hand and put it in my side. Do not doubt but believe." Thomas answered him, "My Lord and my God!" Jesus said to him, "Have you believed because you have seen me? Blessed are those who have not seen and yet have come to believe."

Scripture Commentary

The passage recalls that the disciples were still in hiding because of fear of a possible Jewish backlash after Jesus' execution. They must also have felt some trepidation about what a risen Jesus might say to those who had deserted and denied him. That is why his first gesture and first words when he came among them were so important. Clearly the display of his scars was partly to reassure them that it was really him; but his way of doing this could have been a reproach rather than a gesture of triumph and an invitation to share his joy. So too his words, "Peace be with you," which we find on his lips during many of his appearances. His repeated disclosures to many different individuals and groups must also have served to strengthen their sense of belief.

The gesture of breathing on them seems an echo of Gn 2:7 when Yahweh breathed into the first earthling to give life. Here it is a pledge of new life and acceptance after their failure. This links to his words that bestow on them the Spirit and the gift to forgive (Jn 20:23–24). The implicit message seems to be, now that I have forgiven you, you must go out and do likewise. The little vignette about Thomas seems to convey the same message in an intense and personalized way. Its stress on Jesus' physical wounds accentuates the identity between the one who has suffered and he who stands restored before them. It highlights that Thomas should not have needed a sign, yet his very doubt is the occasion for the cry of affirmation of Jesus' identity ("My Lord and my God") that may have served as the original culmination of John's gospel. At the end of John's passion account Jesus freely yields up his spirit; now we see how this gift has enabled the powerful outpouring of the Spirit of God to bring forgiveness and closure.

Additional Passages ·

Ez 37:1–14	The dry bones shall live.
Is 35:1–10	The Lord will make a way through the wilderness.

Questions for Reflection

1. Have I allowed the Holy Spirit to take away all my shame and guilt, the baggage from my past?
2. What people do I know who are wise in the ways of the Spirit, who could help me in my journeying with God?
3. What is the dominant wind of my region? What important physical and geographic effects does its blowing bring to us who live here?

A Final Thought

I am that living and fiery essence of the divine substance that flows in the beauty of the fields. I shine on the water; I burn in the sun and moon and the stars. The mysterious force of the invisible world is mine. I sustain the breath of all living beings. I breathe in the grass and in the flowers; and when the waters flow like living things, it is I. . . . I am the force that lies hidden in the winds; they take their source from me, as a man may move because he breathes; fire burns by my blast. All these live because I am in them and am their life. I am Wisdom. The blaring thunder of the Word by which all things were made is mine. I permeate all things that they may not die, I am life.

—Hildegard of Bingen

Day 29
Replaying the Past Through New Eyes

Prayer Desire

I ask God for the grace to see the meaning, value, and beauty of my life's story.

Ignatian Focus

What I want is an inner awareness of all the good things I have been given by God, so that I can acknowledge the fullness of his plans for me, and so be able to love and serve God with a full heart. (*The Spiritual Exercises* 233)

Introduction

The Judeo-Christian story offers a unique perspective on time. Most ancient religions viewed time as a ceaseless cycle of birth, ripening, and death by which all nature constantly renewed itself. History was fated and determined; notions of freedom and progress were illusions. The calling of a covenant people by Yahweh initiated a new view of time. God's intervention in human history broke this cycle. It promised a new and better future, freedom for Israel and a new land. The coming of Christ and the definitive action of his passion, death, and resurrection fulfilled the promise to Israel in a totally unexpected way. And it continues to be fulfilled today. Just as Jesus has passed through death to new life with God, so too the church shall follow. For where Jesus, the head of the body, has gone, so will the rest of the members go.

Jesus' resurrection likewise renews the physical world, and as such it points to a renewed cosmos. Because of the resurrection the cosmos has a future that is more than an inevitable heat death or the "big crunch" resulting from a collapsing universe. While humanity awaits the fulfillment of God's promise, it lives in a creative and dynamic space in which human freedom and the indeterminacy of some physical laws allow for a provisional and unfinished character to a universe otherwise ruled by rigid and predictable forces. To some extent, human freedom can shape history and its processes, thus giving men and women a real reason for hope.

The resurrection alters the way we perceive time and its passing. In principle Christ has already triumphed and the destiny of time's arrow is ensured. The entire creation will eventually be taken up into him. Yet how that comes about is open to a myriad of possibilities to be worked out creatively and freely through human decisions as well as the implacable power of cosmic forces. One of the consequences of this in our personal lives is the way in which we can look back on long periods of our lives and suddenly see their meaning and purpose with totally new comprehension. Events and their consequences cannot be changed, but sometimes their significance can alter because they are seen in a new framework. One thinks of Helen Keller's comment about her struggles with her disabilities: "I thank God for my handicaps, for, through them, I have found myself, my work, and my God."

Ecological Reflection

Social commentators point out that some people living in our rapidly changing information-driven society find that their sense of identity and purpose seems very nebulous. The very pace and impact of technological change is a leading factor in this sense of instability. When one's job, career prospects, home, or spouse are subject to unexpected change, it is no wonder that people struggle with a sense of coherent identity. Much of this is linked to the breakdown of local and family communities that is a feature of our society. One of the functions of such communities is to repeat the story of its origins. Retelling where one came from, all the family triumphs and disasters, tales of famous gamblers like Uncle Jim or incredibly hard workers like Cousin Sally give a sense of continuing life and purpose. So it is with the church and the story of Jesus' resurrection. Retelling this story over and over, especially in the liturgy, sets up a framework in which the struggles, disappointments, and hopes of one's own life make sense. And in listening to other people's stories, our own experiences begin to come into clearer focus.

The domination of our society by technology makes such storytelling increasingly difficult. Though the media has brought many distant stories right into the heart of our homes, it is impossible for us to interact with the distant narrator. TV news in particular makes the anchorperson authoritative while the viewer is just a passive spectator. This trend is further accentuated by the advertising industry. Advertising contains almost no information any more; it is almost entirely motivational. Viewers are treated merely as irrational and incompetent consumers. Goods are not sold on the basis of value or beauty, but as enhancements of sexuality, social status, and individualistic "freedom of choice." The ceaseless onslaught on parents (via their children) to buy junk-toys, games, or other products that will be broken, discarded, and forgotten within two to three months is not just damaging to children's sense of values, but to the environment as well. Even more, it creates cynicism and a sense of detachment between people's sense of identity and the stories that frame and shape their world. In a media-saturated culture, our young people can be easily discouraged from developing a spirit of questioning, or can let their imaginations wither as they are constantly bombarded by powerful and persuasive images.

Scripture Reflection: Jn 21:1–14

After these things Jesus showed himself again to the disciples by the Sea of Tiberias; and he showed himself in this way. Gathered there together were Simon Peter, Thomas called the Twin, Nathaniel of Cana in Galilee, the sons of Zebedee, and two others of his disciples. Simon Peter said to them, "I am going fishing." They said to him, "We will go with you." They went out and got into the boat, but that night they caught nothing.

Just after daybreak, Jesus stood on the beach; but the disciples did not know that it was Jesus. Jesus said to them, "Children, you have no fish, do you?" They answered him, "No." he said to them, "Cast the net to the right side of the boat, and you will find some." So they cast it, and now they were not able to haul it in because there were so many fish. That disciple whom Jesus loved said to Peter, "It is the Lord!" When Simon Peter heard that it was the Lord, he put on some clothes, for he was naked, and jumped into the sea. But the other disciples came in the boat, dragging the net full of fish, for they were not far from the land, only about a hundred yards off.

When they had gone ashore, they saw a charcoal fire there, with fish on it, and bread. Jesus said to them, "Bring some of the fish you have just caught." So Simon Peter went aboard and hauled the net ashore, full of large fish, a hundred and fifty three of them; and though there were so many, the net was not torn. Jesus said to them, "Come and have breakfast." Now none of the disciples dared to ask him, "Who are you?" because they knew it was the Lord. Jesus came and took the bread and gave it to them and did the same with the fish. This was now the third time that Jesus appeared to the disciples after he was raised from the dead.

Scripture Commentary

This incident is obviously closely patterned on Lk 5:4 ff., in which Jesus originally calls Simon Peter, his partner (presumably Andrew), James, and John. Jesus reaffirms the same call after so much had changed for the disciples and after they had learned so much about themselves in their attempt to follow him. The incident faithfully records how each disciple is so different in temperament and action: John is insightful and perceptive; Peter is still impetuous and inclined to the grand gesture. The symbolism of the great number of fish, 153, is not clear to scholars, but it speaks of great abundance and surprise. John's solemn language describing the meal on the beach (Jn 21:9–13) clearly has eucharistic overtones. It may help us make sense of the paradox that the disciples are unsure of this stranger yet have no need to ask his identity. They know deeply and instinctively that this is the same Jesus they knew before his death and resurrection. But they are so overawed by what has happened to him that they do not have the courage to ask about it. As this chapter unfolds, it will be Jesus who takes the initiative and puts into a new context what has happened in the past, namely, Peter's betrayal. This will free him and the other disciples to follow Jesus' new call, one that integrates all that had happened to them since they first met him here on the shore of the Sea of Tiberias, and takes it up in a new way.

Additional Passages

Jn 21:15–24   Jesus reaffirms the call of Peter and John.

Mt 28:16–20   Jesus sends out his disciples to preach to all.

Questions for Reflection

1. How has the journey through the Exercises helped me to a fuller sense of my identity and calling?
2. Had I the chance to stand with Jesus on the beach, what might he say to me about my past and my future?
3. Have I been able to integrate the visual media and consumerism in an appropriate way in my life, or do I still need more critical work and control over them?

A Final Thought

On the road above the school
waves a wheatfield.
Tonight its sinuous folds
rippled and swayed
in a sensuous song
of wonder for its maker;
its green-golden sheen
in the late evening air
made it seem
an inland sea
of yellow weave.
A month ago it stood stiff green
spiky in
stalk and leaf.
When was the
moment of transformation?
I did not see
it for looking.
Like the ear
of wheat
am I grown,
ready to be
ground and baked
into the
bread of Christ,
ripe and full,
though all I can recall
is the stalk
drying and dying.

Day 30
A New Creation

Prayer Desire

I ask to see how I can best work for the coming of a new creation where Christ is all in all.

Ignatian Focus

I consider how God toils and labors for me in all created things on this planet—in the heavens, the elements, plants, fruits, flocks, and in all else. He gives existence, preserves, and makes grow. (*The Spiritual Exercises* 236)

Introduction

When I first saw the science-fiction film *Independence Day* about seven years ago, I had two very different reactions. The first was the sense that as a species we have a deep need not to feel alone in the universe. The second was a sense of fear of our vulnerability. What a glow of comfort the film provided, that we could outsmart aliens so far technically superior to ourselves—yet rightly despise them because they were so repulsive and vicious. As a consequence the audience could cheer and feel smugly virtuous as the invaders' enormous craft crashed onto the Nevada mountains, frying millions of the aliens. In many ways science fiction has become the secular equivalent of the apocalyptic books of the Bible. It attempts to answer questions about the end-times of humankind and what will be our ultimate destiny. It is sad that the shallow jingoism of much science fiction and biblical fundamentalism have obscured the profound questions about the destiny of our world that are posed by a book such as John's Revelation.

I think it is true to say that in the Christian tradition the dominant interpretation of Jesus' redemption and resurrection has been private and spiritual; that is, its central focus has been on the inner transformation of the individual. Nevertheless, we must not ignore that within the tradition there has always been a stream that has regarded these events in a far more cosmic light. Its vision is that Christ will come ultimately, in the midst of a deadly struggle with evil, to transform the entire universe, so making God's restoration of creation complete. This vision begins with Paul in Eph 1:3–14 and Col 1:13–20. We find it too in the early fathers of the church, for instance, Irenaeus:

> For the Creator of the world is truly the Word of God: and this is our Lord, who in the last times was made man, existing in this world, and who in an invisible manner contains all things created, and is inherent in the entire creation, since the Word of God governs and arranges all things; and therefore He came to His own in a visible manner, and was made flesh, and hung upon the tree, that He might sum up all things in Himself.

Or take these remarkable words from St. Ambrose: "The world rose in him (Christ), the heavens rose in him, the earth rose in him. For there will be new heavens and a new earth." And this idea of the entire universe being restored in Christ is the central vision of the Book of Revelation, the concluding book of the New Testament.

Ecological Reflection

We have seen how the resurrection of the second Adam in the garden of Golgotha reversed the damage wrought by the first Adam in the Garden of Eden. The restoration of the garden means that Christians can now turn to the task of beautifying and redeeming the city. So many of the new Christian communities sprang up in the great cities of Asia Minor, like Antioch, Ephesus, or Caesarea, then in Europe in Corinth and Rome. The Acts of the Apostles is a tale of many cities and the journeys between them. The final book of the Bible, Revelation, tells of the coming of the new Jerusalem, the heavenly city, which contains all the features of the garden: the sacred river, the medicinal trees, and the healing waters. These images evoke the original Eden, yet have become wedded to human creativity in a city that is a witness both to nature's fertility and to human resourcefulness and work.

Many people living in industrialized societies, mostly in cities, feel trapped. While they are certain that modern work processes are far more efficient than those of twenty or thirty years ago, and they are well aware of the enormous choices they have in leisure products or for trips to exotic tourist destinations, they cannot understand why they constantly feel so exhausted and seem to be working ever harder than before. As we have seen, this perception is true: most are working longer hours for relatively lower returns. The great irony is that our modern culture, dedicated to the pursuit of leisure, has produced a civilization of frantic workers. Having lives shaped by the clock and work demands has led many workers to experience life as feverish, a constant rush from place to place, commitment to commitment, with little sense of serenity or enjoyment of beauty. Because of a diminished sense of providence and of lives resting in God's hands, many feel that the state of the world is wholly a human responsibility. Lives and plans are no longer perceived as growing slowly in God's time but are measured frantically against the inrushing weight of the future. This conviction that humans are creating the future makes it impossible for many to live in the present. The now disappears because it is always being gobbled up before it is born.

In a world that embraced Jesus' resurrection, work would be transformed. Humans would see both the meaning of time and the purpose of work quite differently. The risen Christ has conquered time, and therefore the resurrection allows us to revision our past. It enables us to see God's love, presence, and magical sleight of hand in all sorts of events that we thought were dead for us but have now come back to life in strange and exciting ways. This new understanding of the past also reshapes the future. Knowing how God has reconfigured our past, we sense that the future is an arena of even greater possibilities, no matter the external changes that our lives may pass through. With such a vision, work is distinctively human and spiritual because it is the human contribution to the ongoing transformation of the universe, as well as the place where we unravel our salvation in space and time. Work is both personal and relational, for in our work we know the universe and respond to it, while striving to uncover and tap its fullest potential. Work is built on the original covenant with God, which was a love story. The paradoxical quality of all successful love stories is that they are win-win situations. The more each partner gives, the more satisfying, fulfilling, and life-giving it turns out for both of them. The sum of the outputs is much greater than the individual inputs. This happens because trust and cooperation promote generativity and foster imagination and vision. This stimulates far more growth than extra pay for extra hours will. Workplaces built around this insight would be immeasurably happier and more productive places.

Scripture Reflection: Rv 21:1–7

Then I saw a new heaven and a new earth; for the first heaven and the first earth had passed away, and the sea was no more. And I saw the holy city, the new Jerusalem, coming down out of heaven from God, prepared as a bride adorned for her husband. And I heard a loud voice from the throne saying,

> "See, the home of God is among mortals.
> He will dwell with them;
> they will be his peoples,
> and God himself will be with them;
> he will wipe away every tear from their eyes.
> Death will be no more;
> mourning and crying and pain will be no more,
> for the first things have passed away."

And the one who was seated on the throne said, "See, I am making all things new." Also he said, "Write this, for these words are trustworthy and true." Then he said to me, "It is done! I am the Alpha and the Omega, the beginning and the end. To the thirsty I will give water as a gift from the spring of the water of life. Those who conquer will inherit these things, and I will be their God and they will be my children."

Scripture Commentary

To say that the Apocalypse is a genre of biblical writing closest to our science fiction does not mean it is fantasy. Rather, there are very serious messages, but they are concealed in a semifictional story full of symbols, struggle, and war. Central to the story and its symbolism is the contrast between the heavenly Jerusalem, depicted as a bride, and imperial Rome, depicted as the harlot of Babylon. Implicit in this is a comparison between two different political economies. Imperial Rome was notorious for its environmental injustice (such as massive deforestation) and its ecological imperialism (stripping food and mineral wealth from its conquered territories). This way of life is contrasted with the New Jerusalem, a totally renewed urban world, where God makes his home, in the midst of our world.

Imperial Rome depicted itself in its literature as an empire without end. It dominated global trade through its control of all shipping. This is why the sea will be no more (Rv 21:1), for this domination will come to an end. The exploitation of wealth made possible by this maritime control had created a wasteland in some areas, which were deforested and plundered. In contrast, within the New Jerusalem life and its essentials are given without cost. No sea means no shipping economy, no exploitation, or traffic in cargo. But there will be water; the invitation to drink of the waters (Rv 21:6) is a promise of healing. Water is also a symbol of life-giving fertility and of Wisdom. Contrary to the fundamentalist notion of the faithful being taken up to heaven in "the rapture," it is God who comes down to live in a great city in the midst of a restored creation, a city whose architecture, precious stones, wondrous gates, and gardens are open to all who are part of her.

Additional Passages

Acts 1:1–11   Jesus ascends into heaven.
Col 3:1–4   Our life is hidden with Christ in God.

Questions for Reflection

1. When I think of the end of the world, what images and stories give me a framework for hope?
2. Is my work creative and life-giving, or do I constantly feel rushed, under pressure, and anxious? How could I change this?
3. Is the city in which I live (or one with which I am familiar) a beautiful or ugly place? What strategies could beautify it and make it a humane and gracious place in which to live?

A Final Thought

A friend of God was pondering over the puniness of human beings compared to the immense sweep of this universe, asking how they could be of significance in the vast panoply of creation. It was then that God opened his mind to the entire creation, his vision passing from galaxy to galaxy, an endless sea of exploding suns, a boundless rippling of dark and mysterious seething matter, of stars coming to birth, of pressures and temperatures and immense gravity beyond all human conception. Yet every speck and least mite of this boundless array was fully present to the mind of God, loving and sustaining each tiniest particle. Then it came to him that he too could encompass all this wonder because he too was made in the image of God, he could share the mind of God. In a flash he passed from one universe to another. He was rooted in this earth, one of six billion, a dust mite on this speck of terrestrial matter. Yet all this vision was encompassed in his brain in his fragile skull. In wonder his cry welled up, "O God, how exquisite you are." In silence, a tiny voice replied, "You are exquisite."

CONCLUSION

As with many life-changing experiences, it may take retreatants some months, even a year or two, to come to grips with the extent of the journey they have undertaken in *The Spiritual Exercises*. There are six key areas of transformation in the way retreatants see their lives as a result of the Exercises. The first and most important conviction that the retreatant gains is that God wants each one of us to be deeply joyful because we have been freed from whatever entraps us. There is a heart-felt sense of what Paul says in Rom 6:3–4:

> Do you not know that all of us who have been baptized into Christ Jesus were baptized into his death? Therefore we have been buried with him by baptism into death, so that, just as Christ was raised from the dead by the glory of his Father, so we too might walk in newness of life.

The two vital components in this freedom are love and a shared passage of suffering. In the musical *My Fair Lady* at one stage Eliza gets very frustrated with her admirer Freddy's descriptions of his feelings for her and sings a wonderful song called "Don't Talk of Love, Show Me." Watching with Jesus through his passion and seeing him die give one a profound sense of touching human evil and the power of a great love in overcoming that. Hearing the risen Lord say to Thomas (and to oneself, who is there in spirit), "Put your finger here and see my hands. Reach out your hand and put it in my side. Do not doubt but believe" (Jn 20:27), is like the difference between seeing a beautiful stranger across a crowded room and holding one's beloved in one's arms. Such love is personal, unreserved, and built upon total acceptance of each other.

Another dimension of this new sense of freedom is that it is cast out of the crucible of a shared passage of suffering and acknowledgment of failure. The retreatant has been close to Jesus' struggles with evil and seen the strategies that adulation, power, and desire for the sweet life attempted to weave about Christ to ensnare him, all to no avail. For their part, retreatants are very aware that they have been victims of the same ploys but so often failed to advert to them or happily succumbed to them. There is pain in the awareness of such failures, and the sense that the flaws that enabled such sins to happen are still part of one's life. Now, however, the difference is that these wounds are not just the place that Jesus has touched in his healing but are also the abiding pledge of his continuing presence and support. They are part of the pact of love.

The second fruit of the Exercises is a growing understanding that all of life is a gift from God, even the parts that are painful. Many of us have been carrying since childhood the legacy of a two-faced Janus-God: one of the faces is Jesus our friend; the other is God the accountant. This sense that we must shape up or we will not be accepted and loved can well up from memories of our childhood vulnerability. It also seems to find a mandate in many parts of the Old Testament. One of the meditations often used during the first week of the Exercises that seems to fit this pattern of God's rigorous demands for unquestioning obedience is the famous passage of the sacrifice of Isaac, God's test of Abraham's faith (Gn 22:1–19). It can only be seen for what it is after we have passed through the fourth week. Exegetically and theologically this is a thorny passage. Women retreatants often comment, "What of Sarah's anguish, sitting back at home waiting to hear the outcome, shut out, excluded as women often are from debates that touch the core of their lives and meaning?" When retreatants pose this question, directors may ask them to ponder the "Isaacs" in their lives, those things that they would find hardest to relinquish if God were to ask them. The director then asks them to write their five most precious gifts, possessions, or relationships, each on a single slip of paper. Then in utter honesty in the presence of God to try to yield each one back to God in the reverse order, going from the fifth most important and working up to the most precious belonging, noting what passes through their heart. For many this is beautiful but painful.

What comes out of it is often surprising and illuminating. After sharing the experience, retreatants are then asked to go back and imagine God going through that list but giving each object back to them, saying, "This is my gift of love to you; I want you to receive it with unreserved joy." When this takes place, sometimes retreatants penetrate to a new level of understanding of God's love. They realize that it is not like a checking account where spending on one item makes another unattainable. God's love is like the rays pouring out from the sun. No matter how many creatures absorb them, they are never diminished; there is always more for everyone and everything. The insight given to many retreatants is to realize that God is saying to them, "These things are the gifts of my love, freely given, that you may learn to love. Trust me and I will teach you to love again, but to do this you must unlock your heart and let me have it. I will return it with compound interest, which will be the love of all other things." It is this sort of realization that permits those in the final week to embrace without reservation the prayer of Ignatius that he includes in the Contemplation to Attain the Love of God:

> Take, Lord, and receive all my liberty, my memory, my understanding, and my entire will—all I have and possess. You have given it to me; I return it, Lord, to you. Everything is Yours; dispose of it according to Your will. Give me our love and Your grace; for me, that is enough (*The Spiritual Exercises* 234).

The third fruit of the retreat is to begin to see all the world in God. The Contemplation to Attain the Love of God has a particularly important role here. It keeps on expanding, including all natural things in the sphere of love and beauty. So even the seemingly ordinary, the leaves, the birds on the lawn, the pattern of cloud, sunshine, and rain that is the kaleidoscope of daily weather have wonder and luminosity about them at times. That is so even with the darker side of nature: the millions of eggs that creatures like frogs or fish have to spawn to bring four or five adults to maturity and the predation that sustains so much of the natural world. After passing through Jesus' rising from death, it is easier to see that even the sometimes savage ways of nature have their own beauty and elegance.

The model of Jesus' paschal journey from love, rejection, and death to final vindication and fulfillment is so universal that it can also serve as a template for all the events of life. Those who have made *The Spiritual Exercises* receive an infinitely flexible tool that can be used to shape and make serviceable even the most trivial of experiences. Being forgetful and fallible, they often slip up and let instinctual reservoirs of fear and self-protectiveness dictate their first response. Returning at evening to the few moments of Examen of Consciousness (one of the strategies learned in the retreat), they can recall the episodes where they failed to identify the Jesus who walked through their life at that moment and whose presence they missed. This is not an episode in recrimination, but a moment of healing love, a second bite at the cherry of loving awareness.

Having tasted the generative power of God's love, that grace is a dynamic that can overcome and reverse the entropy of our world, the retreatant is frequently moved to become a disciple in his or her own turn. Many of those who do the thirty-day retreat use it as the springboard for a deepening or refocusing of their mission in life. Some will discover that they misread where they believed God was calling them. Others will go back to their former work with renewed vision and vigor while some will feel the call to a new and often more generous consecration of their lives to God. Sometimes retreatants will discern themselves as being drawn toward work as a spiritual director or retreat giver.

A fourth grace of the retreat is to grasp the mutuality of love, its need both to give and receive. Ignatius was by temperament a very practical man. He notes in several places that real love is shown in actions, not words. Even with Christ our love is always mutual. The Exercises often teach of our call to support Jesus, follow him, and stand under his banner to be his champion, while he has pledged never to leave us. Such reciprocity in loving is healthy and life-giving. But for the codependent who has scripted his life to be the tireless helper or the remorseless worker, allowing oneself to be loved without any strings or expectations is a fearsome new revelation. For the person who has cast his or her life in the victim role and has become addicted to counseling or endless new therapies, acknowledging that he or she is free to give up these roles sufficiently enough to see, hear, and reach out to other people simply because they are in need can be a similar startling and liberating discovery.

Another surprising but important outcome of the retreat is a deep conviction of the centrality of embodiment in Christian life. This is linked to the sacramental dimensions of Christ's transcending of space and time to touch us through our bodies in the embrace of his body at the eucharist. It is the sense in which we realize that his grace and beauty is manifest throughout the entire cosmos and in the apparently blind workings of evolution. Most unexpected though, in such an ascetic saint as Ignatius, is the key role he gives to the body in the art of discernment. Discernment is the very heart of *The Spiritual Exercises*, for it is the rudder that keeps on pointing the ship unerringly toward Christ, its final landfall. Though it requires attentiveness and reflection, discernment is not primarily an intellectual skill. It is the art of monitoring the movements of the heart, the subtlest shifts of longing, rejection, withdrawal, or quickening, that is its métier. As modern psychology insists, the movement of the heart is most often through the language of the body. A tightening of the solar plexus, a clenching of the bowels, a jabbing at the temples is often our first warning, long before our minds have told us that trouble is looming. Symbols from the unconscious are often precursors to insights in the reason. Listening to our hearts and bodies will frequently tell us when we are acting against our basic values and belief systems, at the very time we are concocting elaborate reasons to justify our course of action.

In her examination of Ignatian spirituality, Monica Hellwig has identified five characteristics that make it a superb tool for work in the areas of the struggle for justice in the world today. They serve as an excellent summary of what retreatants will take away as the fruits of a deep engagement in the four weeks of the Exercises:

- a grounding of everything in profound gratitude and reverence
- a continuous cultivation of critical awareness
- a confident expectation of an empowerment to accept and exercise responsibility

- an unequivocal commitment to action
- the recognition that the gospel of Jesus Christ is essentially countercultural and revolutionary in a nonviolent way

The sixth and final gift of *The Spiritual Exercises* is their capacity to bring about integration deep within those who make them. This will differ depending on the openness and capacity of each retreatant. This is the integration of three different ways of understanding the world, and the unifying of three stories: God's love for each person, human understanding of God's revelation (theology), and the scientific account of our earthly origins, all of which are intertwined and shape one another. The fruit of Ignatius's final exercise, the Contemplation to Attain the Love of God, is to see God's love in every event of life and in all of creation.

Such an approach goes far beyond intellectual constructions; it demands a humble and persistent effort to constrain the egotism that consistently tends to overrate personal importance and so control and manipulate other people as well as nature for purely selfish reasons. On the other hand, such integration requires the faith to believe that God's personal love for oneself is so immense that every moment and every circumstance of life is pregnant with God's presence and promise. It is possible to maintain such a stance when nature, science, and theology are all seen as expressions of the all-enveloping love of God. Such a vision will allow one to surrender to the transcendence of God on the heights of Mt. Everest, to see the divine delicacy in the perfect nautilus shell cast up on the shore, or to have a sense of the loving purpose of evolution when looking at the layers of multicolored volcanic sands from Rainbow Mountain in New Zealand's Bay of Plenty. At such a moment one can be profoundly struck by the observation made by William Blake in his *Auguries of Innocence*, from which the title of this book suggested itself to me:

> To see a World in a Grain of Sand
> And a Heaven in a Wild Flower,
> Hold Infinity in the palm of your hand
> An Eternity in an hour.

SOURCES

Numerous books and articles have helped shape my thought. I have acknowledged them when cited directly in the text. We wanted, however, to avoid turning this prayer journey into a theological treatise, and so references have been kept to a minimum. I am aware that over a decade of compiling material through three generations of computers I have lost track of the sources of a few of my seminal ideas. I apologize to any author who has accidentally been overlooked because of this. In the areas of science and theology I do want to single out just a few of the many authors whose works have been important for me:

Austin, Richard. *Beauty of the Lord*. Louisville, Ky.: John Knox Press, 1988.
_____. *Hope for the Land*. Louisville, Ky.: John Knox Press, 1988.
Banks, Robert. *God the Worker: Journeys Into the Mind, Heart, and Imagination of God*. Sutherland, New South Wales, Australia: Albatross Books, 1992.
Barbour, Ian. *Religion in the Age of Science*. San Francisco: HarperCollins, 1990.
Behe, Michael. *Darwin's Black Box*. New York: Simon and Schuster, 1996.
Beisner, Calvin E. *Where Garden Meets Wilderness*. Grand Rapids, Mich.: Eerdmans, 1997.
Brungs, Robert, and Marianne Postiglione, general editors. *ITEST Publications and Conferences*. St. Louis: Institute for Theological Encounter with Science and Technology, 1991–2002.
Charbonneaus-Lassay, Louis. *The Bestiary of Christ*. New York: Parabola Books, 1991.
Denton, Michael. *Nature's Destiny*. New York: Free Press, 1998.
Diamond, Jared. *The Rise and Fall of the Third Chimpanzee*. London: Vintage, 1991.
Eldredge, Niles. *Life in the Balance*. Princeton, N.J.: Princeton University Press, 1998.
Gould, Stephen. *Wonderful Life: The Burgess Shale and the Nature of History*. London: Penguin, 1991.
Hall, Douglas. *Imaging God: Dominion as Stewardship*. Grand Rapids, Mich.: Eerdmans, 1986.

Haught, John. *God After Darwin: A Theology of Evolution.* Boulder, Colo.: Westview, 2000.

_____. *The Promise of Nature.* Mahwah, N.J.: Paulist Press, 1993.

Hough, Adrian. *God Is Not Green: A Re-examination of Eco-theology.* Leominster, England: Gracewing, 1997.

James, David. *What Are They Saying About Masculine Spirituality?* Mahwah, N.J.: Paulist Press, 1996.

Klein, Naomi. *No Logo.* London: Flamingo, 2001.

Leopold, Aldo. *A Sand County Almanac.* New York: Ballantine Books, 1976.

Lilburne, Geoffrey. *A Sense of Place: A Christian Theology of the Land.* Nashville: Abingdon Press, 1989.

McFague, Sallie. *Super, Natural Christians: How We Should Love Nature.* London: SCM, 1997.

McKibben, Bill. *The End of Nature.* London: Penguin, 1990.

Midgley, Mary. *The Ethical Primate.* London: Routledge, 1996.

Murray, Robert. *The Cosmic Covenant.* London: Sheed and Ward, 1992.

Park, Geoff. *Nga Uruora, the Groves of Life: Ecology and History in a New Zealand Landscape.* Wellington, Victoria: University Press, 1995.

Petty, Michael. *A Faith That Loves the Earth: The Ecological Theology of Karl Rahner.* Lanham, Md.: University Press of America, 1996.

Rifkin, Jeremy. *The End of Work.* New York: G. P. Putnam's Sons, 1996.

Schama, Simon. *Landscape and Memory.* Toronto: Vintage Canada, 1996.

Waddell, Helen. *Beasts and Saints.* Grand Rapids, Mich.: Eerdmans, 1996.

Watson, Lyall. *Dark Nature.* New York: HarperCollins, 1995.

Wilkinson, Loren. *Earthkeeping in the Nineties.* Grand Rapids, Mich.: Eerdmans, 1991.

As far as material on *The Spiritual Exercises* and St. Ignatius are concerned, the works and translations of Herbie Alphonso, Tad Dunne, John English, David Fleming, Jean Laplace, and David Stanley have all been significant. Quotations from *The Spiritual Exercises of St. Ignatius* have been taken from the translation by David Fleming (St. Louis: Institute of Jesuit Resources, 1978) or from the translation by George Ganss (St. Louis: Institute of Jesuit Resources, 1992). On some occasions I have paraphrased these excerpts. Of all the works I have drawn upon in this area, however, the most useful for my work has been Joseph Tetlow's *Choosing Christ in the World* (St. Louis: Institute of Jesuit Resources, 1989).The numeral referred to in *The Spiritual Exercises* is the paragraph number.

Sources quoted in the text are as follows:

To Hold Infinity in the Palm of Your Hand
Gaston Bachelard, *La terre et les reveries du repos* (N.p.: José Certi, 1948).

Week One
Jonathan Edwards, *Charity and Its Fruits* (N.p.,1969), pp. 157–58.

Robert Banks, *God the Worker* (Sutherland, Australia: Albatross Books, 1992), p. 387.

Day 1

Richard Rohr, "Christianity and the Creation," in *Embracing Earth*, A. LaChance and J. Carroll, ed. (Maryknoll, N.Y.: Orbis, 1994), p. 142.

Day 2

The Endeavour Journal of Sir Joseph Banks, 1768–71, entry of 17 January 1770.

Day 3

Joseph Tetlow, *Choosing Christ in the World* (St. Louis: Institute of Jesuit Sources, 1989), p. 128; as altered by Neil Vaney.

Day 4

Armenian Prayer for Epiphany, quoted in Vigen Gurion, *Communio* 18 (spring 1991): 98–99.

Day 5

The prayer in "A Final Thought" is by the author.

Day 6

Thomas Merton, *Conjectures of a Guilty Bystander* (New York: Doubleday, 1965).

Day 7

James Jeans, *The Mysterious Universe* (Cambridge: Cambridge University Press, 1931).

Day 8

C. S. Lewis, *The Magician's Nephew* (New York: HarperCollins, 1994).

Day 9

Bernard Schlink, *The Reader* (New York: Vintage International, 1998).

Day 10

Robert Banks *God the Worker* (Sutherland, Australia: Albatross Books, 1992).

Day 11

Karl Rahner, *Theological Investigations* (Baltimore: Helicon Press, 1961), p. 111.

Day 12

The poem in "A Final Thought" is by the author.

Day 13

James Irwin, *An Introduction to Maori Religion* (Bedford Park, South Australia: Australian Association for the Study of Religion, 1984), p. 7.

Day 14

Ishpriya, *Earth Prayers* (San Francisco: HarperSanFrancisco, 1991), p. 164.

Day 15

Margaret Atwood, *The Handmaid's Tale* (Boston: Houghton and Mifflin, 1984), p 165.
Henry David Thoreau, "Walking," from *Excursions* (1863).

Day 16
Moses Cordovero, source unknown.

Day 17
Diane Fasel, *Working Ourselves to Death* (San Francisco: HarperCollins, 1990), pp. 2, 9.

Day 18
George Appleton, in *The Oxford University Book of Prayer,* ed. George Appleton (New York: Oxford University Press), 1985.

Day 19
Source unknown.

Day 20
Michael Mott, *The Seven Mountains of Thomas Merton* (New York: Houghton Mifflin Co, 1984), p. 554.

St. Bonaventure, quoted in Zachary Hayes, *The Gift of Being* (Collegeville, Minn: Liturgical Press, 2000), pp. 106–7.

Day 21
William Vanstone, *Love's Endeavour, Love's Expense*, quoted in John Polkinghorne *Scientists as Theologians: The Search for Understanding* (London: SPCK, 1988), p. 62.

Day 22
The poem in "A Final Thought" is by the author.

Day 23
Source unknown.

Day 25
Erik Erikson, speaking of the importance of models to children, in *Childhood and Society* (1963).

Day 26
The poem in "A Final Thought" is by the author.

Day 27
John Soos, "To be of the Earth is to know," *Earth Prayers* (San Francisco: Harper San Francisco, 1991), p 288.

Day 28
Source unknown.

Day 29
The poem in "A Final Thought" is by the author.

Day 30
The story in "A Final Thought" is by the author.

Photo by Patrick Bellett Photography at www.phototime.co.nz

Neil Vaney, SM, is a lecturer in Christian ethics at Good Shepherd College, Auckland, New Zealand. He holds an M.A. from the University of Canterbury, an S.T.L. from Gregorian University in Rome, and a Ph.D. from the University of Otago.

He has written articles for a variety of publications and has contributed to five previous books, including *Catholic Dictionary of Social Justice,* and *Human Rights and the Common Good*. He resides in Grafton, Auckland, New Zealand.

More Spiritual Favorites

Moment By Moment
A Retreat in Everyday Life
Carol Ann Smith, SHCJ & Eugene F. Merz, SJ
ISBN: 0-87793-945-4 / 96 pages / $11.95

Drawing on the classic retreat model, *The Spiritual
Exercises of St. Ignatius*, **Moment by Moment** offers a
new and inviting way to find God in our often busy
and complex lives. Its simple format can be used by an
individual or by groups.

Paying Attention to God
Discernment in Prayer
William A. Barry, SJ
ISBN: 0-87793-413-4 / 128 pages / $9.95

"I am convinced," says Barry, "that we encounter God in a
mysterious way and that God wants a personal relationship
with each of us." Helping people pay attention to these
encounters is the purpose of this book.

Opening to God
A Guide to Prayer
Thomas H. Green, SJ
ISBN: 0-87793-136-4 / 112 pages / $9.95

A book that uncomplicates prayer for both the beginner
and the experienced prayer. **Opening to God** is a unique
combination of fundamentals, fully grounded in the tradition
of the Christian mystics, plus a wealth of "today" insights
into what is really involved in laying the foundations of a
genuine life of prayer.

Earth's Echo
Sacred Encounters with Nature
Robert M. Hamma
ISBN: 1-893732-46-0 / 192 pages / $12.95

Earth's Echo is a book for people who love nature and find
spiritual meaning in it. Anyone who looks and notices what
they see can find God in the world around them. **Earth's
Echo** leads readers to reflect on the sacred reality of nature
as found in different settings: the seashore, the river, the
forest, the desert, and the mountains.

KEYCODE: FØTØ1Ø4ØØØØ